The Six Keys:
Strategies for Promoting Children's Mental Health in Early Childhood Programs

The Six Keys:
Strategies for Promoting Children's Mental Health

Sparrow Media Group
Farmington, Minnesota

Library of Congress Cataloging-in-Publication Data

Croft, Cindy.
  The six keys : strategies for promoting children's mental health / by Cindy Croft.
-- 1st ed.
    p. cm.
  ISBN-13: 978-0-9786018-2-9
  ISBN-10: 0-9786018-2-3
  1. Emotions in children. 2. Child psychology. I. Title.

BF723.E6C76 2007
155.4--dc22

                                        2006030310

Book and cover design by Avallo   www.avallo.com
Printed and bound in the United States.
First edition, 2007.

Quantity discounts are available for organizations or universities.
Contact:
Sparrow Media Group
16588 Fieldcrest Avenue, Farmington, MN 55024
Phone: 952-953-9166 • Fax: 952-431-3461
info@sparrowmediagroup.com • www.sparrowmediagroup.com

Contents

Introduction

The purpose of this book is to support the work of early-childhood professionals caring for young children in a variety of settings. Information included here will help child-care practitioners and educators to become more aware of the importance of emotional development for children. Promoting positive mental health in young children begins in infancy with responsive caregiving by the important people in a baby's life and proceeds through early childhood with consistent and quality nurturing and caregiving. The role of the child-care provider and early educator is primary in ensuring the best possible outcomes for children's social and emotional health through the developmentally appropriate activities and environment provided. Consistent observation and recording may reveal to a child-care practitioner indicators of risk in a child's emotional development. While a child-care provider has a responsibility to refer parents as necessary to local early intervention resources, the role of the provider is not one of a mental health professional in the identification or diagnosis of mental health issues. The child-care provider is there in support of a child's overall emotional well-being as it pertains to the child care setting.

The Six Keys: Strategies for Promoting Children's Mental Health in Early Childhood Programs provides support to early childhood practitioners through training and educational opportunities around the emotional development of children. It is a holistic approach that helps practitioners examine their role in children's mental health, as well as the role of environment, temperament, risk factors, and resilience.

Each chapter includes:

Wisdom from the Field, offering the expertise and experience of early childhood educators from across the country who were part of a university teacher preparation program from 2001-2006. Their input provides strategies for effective practices.

Key Points capture the essential information in each chapter.

Childhood Vignettes appear in italics throughout the book to emphasize the ongoing nature of emotional development in day-to-day experiences that children have.

Some style issues:

He and **she** are used interchangeably throughout the text in an effort to be respectful of both genders.

Caregiver, practitioner, provider, teacher, educator are used interchangeably to refer to the early childhood professional working in a setting that provides early care and education to young children, birth to age eight. This includes family childcare, child-care centers, nursery schools, school readiness programs, Head Start classrooms and other similar settings. Any names used are fictional and examples are a composite of experiences of the author.

Different cultural approaches to child rearing can impact the relationship of the parent to the early childhood professional when it comes to emotional milestones and development. Attachment, temperament, family systems, and risk factors all need to be viewed with cultural respect and awareness. Ultimately, all children need to feel safe and secure in their early childhood setting and we can assure this outcome if we work closely with families, building a relationship of trust through open and honest communication.

Chapter 1

Why All the Fuss About a Child's Emotional Development?

Key 1: Provide responsive caregiving.

So How Are the Children?

What is it about the emotional development of young children that has triggered so much interest by researchers and early childhood experts in the last few years? People in the early childhood care field—teachers, child care providers, policy makers—have many questions about whether we are doing right by children in our practices and our programs when it comes to children's mental health. What is going on in our families and our communities that prompts so much study and reflection? Is it because we see children in the news who have committed unimaginable crimes against themselves and others and we can't understand why? Is it because there is an increase in earlier and younger diagnosis of conditions like depression and emotional/behavioral disorders in young children? Or, is it that our children are spending increasingly more time away from family–in school, activities, child care–and we worry about what that legacy will mean? We are learning a great deal through early childhood research about how children's emotional growth occurs and what can go wrong with that development as it impacts a child's mental health.

> We live in a world in which we need to share responsibility. It's easy to say 'It's not my child, not my community, not my world, not my problem.' Then there are those who see the need and respond. I consider those people my heroes.   --Fred Rogers

The World We Live In

Our world today is often not the place we might have hoped it would be for raising our children. Television in the 1950s presented idealized dramas on television depicting worse-case-scenarios of Beaver Cleaver cheating on a homework assignment, or, in the 1980's, the Huxtable's on "The Cosby Show" in affable family squabbles. But today's television news can shock our senses, like an April 2004 CNN headline that read "Children on Easter Egg Hunt Find Guns Instead" (www.cnn.com, April 11, 2004). We expect children to go to a park and participate in games and fun, not stumble on a loaded weapon. On any given day, we hear current events that make us wonder how we can ever raise capable, successful children. More than not, our culture seems at odds with our values. We see and hear our communities besieged with violence, division, and, sometimes, inhumanity. Caring, involved adults are asking important questions about how we can bring up children in our world who will experience childhood in such a way as to help them be happy and successful as both children and adults.

Many early childhood advocates have used the traditional story of the Masai tribe of Kenya as a rallying cry for changes in our national policies toward children. Masai warriors, as they returned from battle, would enter their villages asking one question: "So how are the children?" They believed that if the children were healthy and cared for, then the community would be strong. For a time, many cars in the U.S. were seen with *So How Are the Children?* bumper stickers. And how are the children? Many would believe that in the 21st century, they are not faring so well.

Five-year-old Sarah is playing with a doll family when her caregiver sits down by her. They begin to talk and Sarah relates that she misses her dad a lot (her parents have been separated for several months). Miss Claire says, "I know it makes you sad not to see your dad." Sarah replies, "My mom won't let me talk to him at all, she is so mad at him. I don't even tell her how much I wish I could go over to his house."

For many children like Sarah, stressors from within the family itself are impacting how they see the world and their relationship to it. In the midst of an often uncertain world, we realize the role healthy emotional development plays in securing well-being for our children. The mental health side of child development has not always been a consideration. Laura Berk, a leading child development expert, explains that for many years the importance of how children learned cognitively overshadowed the emotional side to their development, and now there is great excitement generated within the early childhood field around the mental health of children. *Great excitement* around learning what makes children react the way they do to the world around them, what helps them make and keep friends, what helps them grow into successful adults with healthy relationships (Berk, 1997). We in the early childhood field have felt this excitement too, as we watch children grow and learn about their own feelings and how those feelings relate to others. We see the important role that emotions play in the overall development of a child.

Josh ran into the preschool room yelling, "Everybody hates me, they hate me." He plopped down on a chair and put his head on the table. His teacher sat next to him and said, "I like you Josh," and Huda from across the table said, "I like you, too, Josh."

What do we mean when we talk about children's mental health? Psychologists consider the term *mental health* to refer to "psychological well-being" that takes into account family and interpersonal relationships, as well as relationship to the larger community. Some experts define mental health as the absence of mental illness (Encarta, 2006), but many psychologists consider this definition too narrow. In simple terms, mental health refers to the way children feel about themselves and the world around them. Child developmentalists commonly define mental health for infants as the developing capacity of a baby to experience and regulate their emotions, to form secure attachments and relationships, and to explore their environment (Zero to Three, 2006). As children continue to grow and develop, positive mental health begins to include how they look at themselves and the other people in their lives, and then what they do with that information. It also includes how children relate to others, to challenges, to stress, and to decision-making. Emotional health has a direct impact on how one thinks, learns, communicates, and grows.

This text will use the terms *mental health* and *emotional development* interchangeably, referring to the both the developmental process and the outcome. In this context, emotional development is a major development domain alongside social, cognitive, and physical development and not viewed in a deficit model, as in mental illness. The national nonprofit organization Zero to Three, a primary source on infant growth and development, views mental health as synonymous with healthy social and emotional development. In fact, a child's emotional development begins at the point his innate temperament begins to be recognized. His temperament plays a role in this development along with his environment; if he has had secure attachments as an infant to a primary caregiver, he will see his world as a safe, secure place (Koralek, 1999). The secure attachments come from warm and sensitive caregiving that includes responsiveness and comfort from a consistent caregiver and needs to continue through the preschool years as well. The mental health of a young child is critically tied to who he is naturally and to his early relationships with important caregivers. If we want to ensure that children feel good about themselves and respond positively to the world around them, we need to safeguard their early experiences with their primary caregivers. Early childhood practitioners have a significant role in ensuring healthy emotional development in young children.

The Central Role of Emotions in Human Experience

Given the importance of the early experiences of young children, many child development experts support the explosion of research that maintains that emotions play a central role in all aspects of human experiences (Berk, 1997). *This is a bold statement.* If we believe the research, then consider the ramifications. What does this mean as we examine the experiences we have with children? Does a child who is shy really have a harder time making friends? And if making friends is difficult, how will that impact other activities like learning to share or trust in others? Does trust in others tie in to how well the little one will learn once she is in school? If learning is difficult because the social strata are difficult to navigate, what becomes of this young child's potential? A child's emotional strengths or weaknesses will fundamentally affect how she perceives the world around her and thereby impacts how she will develop socially, physically, and cognitively, as well as in an overall sense of well being. In today's world, school readiness should have more to do with how we nurture a child in their growth toward self-awareness, their ability to regulate their feelings, and their responses to emotions than in their knowing the alphabet. When it comes to the positive mental health of young children, responsive and secure caregiving from infancy to early childhood by a loving adult will have far greater impact than the ability of the child to recite the alphabet before he goes to kindergarten.

School Readiness

The importance of children being ready to learn by the time they reach kindergarten is an important political goal in the 21st century. While there are many dimensions to school readiness, it is important to note research supporting the notion that a child's emotional competence is an important indicator of how ready a child will be to make the key transition to kindergarten. Emotional competence is also an indicator of academic success later on. According to Peth-Pierce (2001), research shows that "social and emotional school readiness is critical to a successful kindergarten transition, early school success, and even later accomplishments in the workplace." She further points out that children who fail early on in school often experience emotional and behavioral problems later in school, further escalating their risk for mental health issues. In a study done for the University of North Carolina, almost half of the kindergarten teachers queried reported that more than 50% of their students had specific behavioral problems in several areas as they readied for first grade (Peth-Pierce, 2001). Among issues that may impact young children as they enter school are the lack of self-regulation skills, social competencies, foundations of trust, and healthy expression of feelings. Healthy emotional development for a child entering kindergarten includes the ability to self-regulate their emotions so they can get along with others and be ready to learn. Children need to have responsive caregiving in order to develop trust in others, a cornerstone of relationships. Healthy emotional development also includes understanding and using an emotional vocabulary that helps children communicate and empathize with others. The mastery of emotional developmental milestones helps prepare a child to effectively learn new cognitive and social skills as they enter school.

What Difference Can We Make?

And so to the early childhood educator, the next questions must be: What do children need from us to be successful in life? Are there fundamental building blocks? How do their educators, caregivers, and parents give them the necessary tools and skills to best enhance social and emotional growth? In order to answer these questions, we need to understand what emotional development is in the life of a child, how it occurs, what influences it, and our roles in nurturing it.

Wisdom from the Field

Early childhood educators in a university teacher preparation program were asked how they set up their child care environment for positive emotional support. Here are their strategies:

1. Provide warmth and love in a nurturing atmosphere.
2. Provide a few "get-away" spaces or areas that give a child a place to relax or regroup but are still visible by a teacher.
3. Maintain a calm and relaxing atmosphere in the program that resists loud noise or inappropriate activity.
4. Create an atmosphere that reflects each child's home culture including families, language, foods, and toys.
5. Make sure there are a range of materials for all age and developmental levels, making challenge as well as success and proficiency an everyday occurrence.

6. Include games, activities, and dramatic play equipment that support a child's sense of self as well as encourage exploration and creativity.

7. Promote cooperation and group play through materials and activities.

8. Build an atmosphere of respect and acceptance of differences, celebrating uniqueness.

Three-year-old Kimberly throws her favorite bedtime pillow out the car window as her parents drive through Yellowstone Park. Perhaps she was curious about what would happen if she stuck it out the window. Whatever her reason, later at bedtime she is inconsolable when she does not have her pillow to sleep with. It was her security, her support. Mom and Dad try to find other objects to take the place of the pillow. Finally, with Mom singing a soft song, Kimberly falls asleep.

Key 1: Provide responsive caregiving.

Early childhood educators and caregivers, partnering with parents, are in an influential position to help children reach their full potential through strong intentionality about supporting emotional development. If caregivers are knowledgeable about emotional stages and milestones, and have tools to enhance development at each stage, each child can make strong gains. We can nurture the emotional development of young children by our relationships, our practices, and our examples. Even the words we use can be a tool for helping children learn about themselves and their relationship to the rest of the world. Our modeling of language, self-control, empathy, and relationship support becomes essential in helping children reach and master important emotional milestones which is the cornerstone of positive mental health.

How Growth Takes Place

Most early childhood professionals have a broad understanding of the physical stages of development and the corresponding milestones. Ask a roomful of child care providers when children typically begin to use simple sentences, or when they can stand alone or walk, and they will give you an accurate range. But ask the same group when children develop self-awareness, or self-control, and you may find a quiet room. This is not an indictment of the field; it is rather to say that not enough opportunities have been available to practitioners to learn more about this important area of development. According to a leading child developmentalist, emotional development is a major factor in all areas of human activity, including cognitive processing, social behavior, and physical health (Berk, 1997). Many early childhood practitioners have a solid base of physical and cognitive developmental knowledge, but the pervasiveness of the emotional development of children in these other arenas may not be as notable to them. A child who is not meeting emotional development milestones may not be able to achieve his full potential in cognitive and physical development. Mental health is important to us as early childhood professionals because it ultimately defines how a child comes to "feel okay" about his relationship with the rest of his world. Emotional development is not linear in the way we see other childhood development. It involves a learning process called "scaffolding," in which children become engaged by one thing that builds into something more sophisticated or interesting to them, keeping learning ongoing and enriching. A supporting framework launches the exploration of new ideas and development. In emotional development, we see the scaffolding of reactions, feelings, and responsiveness from others into more complex emotional growth. A child learns empathy, for example, through a series of emotional passages. At birth an infant will have an immature reaction to the crying of other infants near her and will cry along; as a toddler, she learns to maneuver through a social context with other toddlers; she feels what it is like to be bit by a peer; as a preschooler she will console a friend who has fallen from a jungle gym. Empathy is not so much the result but rather the process of learning how we interact with the world around us. Positive nurturing between these stages of growth enables a child to grow into an empathetic adult.

Edgar is 5 and is big brother to Sam, who is 7 months. Lying on the floor next to each other, they exchange a series of laughs and sounds and smiling eyes. Edgar blows on his brother's tummy because it makes him laugh. He tells his caregiver, "He likes it when I make this noise." The caregiver sits next to them, laughing along with them. She says, "Edgar, you know just how to make your brother happy. His eyes are looking for your eyes."

In this book, our interest will be in the aspects of a child's emotional development as it is interrelated to the total development of young children. The underpinning of this framework comes from Dr. Ross Thompson (2001), who describes development in these four delineations:

1. The growth of the body (physical size, motor coordination, health).
2. The growth of the mind (thinking, language, concepts, problem solving).
3. The growth of the brain (development of neurons, synapses, and the influence of experience on brain growth).
4. The growth of the person (relationships, social understanding, emotions).

We will comprehensively examine "the growth of the person" as we look at how to encourage and enhance the positive mental health of infants, toddlers, and young children. Who these little people will grow up to be has much to do with the influences in their lives by their primary caregivers, both inside and outside of the home. If children are told they are wonderful beings, and we model to them that we believe they are wonderful, they will have a sense of their own wonder.

What is the Role of Emotions?

Today many early childhood theorists subscribe to the functionalist approach to emotions, which says simply that the function of any emotion is to prompt action to reach a personal goal. From early infancy, we see that children will express an emotion (crying) to receive a personal goal (comfort). Also, other people may help prompt the emotion: a person talking loudly can frighten a baby, making her cry for safety or avoidance of the fearsome person. The same is true for an older preschooler who realizes that screaming loudly in a grocery store checkout line may get him a bag of cookies. Functionalists also refer to another function of emotions as one tied to sensations, so a pleasant smell may evoke an emotional response based on a good experience. Functionalists see emotions as impacting all parts of a person's growth and development. It is difficult to remove an emotion from a given event of learning or growth, as they intertwine so closely. Using one's emotions to gain a personal goal becomes more sophisticated with age and experience. Having a strong awareness of emotions helps us achieve goals for ourselves throughout life, with a process that began in our infancy.

In a classroom, we might see a toddler become frustrated with a puzzle because he lacks some spatial awareness skills. As he practices, and with some assistance from a caregiver, the child can learn to place the correct shaped piece in the corresponding place. The child is intrinsically motivated to succeed; as he gains success, that feeling of accomplishment helps him move on to more sophisticated skill development. He is beginning to learn to control his emotions as he seeks to gain a goal. Again, in a responsive environment where a child has learned that her needs get met when emotions are expressed, the child will feel secure and will be able to move to other levels of emotional growth.

Toddlers often express emotions through their behaviors as part of an emotional vocabulary. Typically, by the time a child is three years old, aggressiveness greatly declines because the child has learned to navigate the social scene, understands consequences to actions, and with support, negotiate with others. As we saw earlier in the chapter, the functionalist approach to emotional development supposes that emotions have as a fundamental role the attainment of personal goals. So, a young child cries in order to get food, or attention, or a hug. The use of emotions in pursuit of personal goals becomes more sophisticated as a child grows and increases his emotional range as well as his cognitive and social skills. Our role as early childhood educators is to teach each child what their emotions mean and, using an emotional vocabulary, to increase each child's healthy use and regulation of emotions from the simple to the complex. (See Chapter 7.)

What Impacts Mental Health Development?

The human drive to develop is inborn, from before birth, and all children are wired to learn and to grow physically, cognitively, socially, and emotionally. The experiences of young children either enhance or inhibit this potential for development (Thompson, 2001). For emotional growth, children in a responsive, nurturing environment will be more apt to thrive. The contrary can also be true. A child in an unresponsive, hostile, or apathetic environment will have difficulty developing strong emotional skills.

Karr-Morse and Wiley (1997) make the case that, in fact, the emotional well being of a child is so greatly influenced by environment that:

> *There does appear to be some evidence that people with certain biological vulnerabilities born into high-risk environments are more likely to act in violent ways. For example, scientists hypothesize that people who are born with relatively "low arousal" or nervous systems that are slow to reach a point of emotional excitement are more able to face risky situations with minimal stress. A child with such qualities might in one environment develop into a race car driver or a stockbroker, and in another, turn to robbing convenience stores. (p. 80)*

In supporting healthy emotional growth in a young child, we must carefully scrutinize the child-care environment for optimal opportunities for safety, exploration, creativity, and community for each child.

The Role of Child Care

As we look at the role that the environment plays in the emotional stages of development, we must factor in the importance of where many children are spending the bulk of their day. Over sixty percent of children aged birth to five years spend some part of their day in an early childhood setting. At one time, the question was whether children should even *be* in child care, if the setting outside of the home was harmful to their development. Twenty years of research has answered that question: non-maternal care does not harm children (Bornstein, 2006). In fact, research overwhelmingly shows us that children in quality settings "show no signs of harm and children from low income families may actually show improved cognitive development" (Phillips, 1987). Today, the non-maternal setting may be in a neighbor's house, a preschool, family child-care program, or licensed child-care center. In many cases, the child-care setting becomes an extension of the home as a part of the larger community that supports children. "It takes a village to raise a child" is an ideal truly lived out as parents and children weave their lives from home to child care to neighborhood and school.

However, we need to consider carefully what the village offers young children. For instance, how a setting "fits" the child is important to his learning key social and emotional skills. Is the child-care program intentional in its practices to enhance strong and positive mental health? Is the emotional environment that a child is experiencing supportive? These questions are important because they have long-term ramifications for children. Research indicates that a child who has not made a significant friend by age six is at risk for delinquency, mental illness issues, and dropping out of school (Wolfe, 2004). Child-care professionals must have an understanding of the emotional needs of young children so they can enhance their social skills as well. A child's difficulty with self-regulation, for example, will impact whether other children want to play with him. A child who frequently has angry outbursts or who doesn't share will have difficulty maintaining friendships. Chapter 4 discusses tools to help children increase their own emotional regulation skills.

Jasmine, age 3, was content to play alone with the people figures in the dollhouse. She moved the 'mom' into the bedroom where the 'baby' was crying. The 'mom' picked up 'baby' and sang a soft song that Jasmine's mom often sang to her.

Quality Does Matter

At this point, it is relevant to talk about the quality of early childhood programs and how that quality, or lack of it, impacts the important emotional stages of each child's life. Many research studies in recent years have looked at the correlation between the quality of early childhood experiences and its relationship to children's healthy emotional development. Westby (Croft and Hewitt, 2004) reiterates the importance of the quality of a setting:

> *Each day of a young child's life is an opportunity to promote the child's growth and development toward becoming a healthy, contributing member of larger society. For many of today's young children, part of this development is taking place as a result of their experiences in an early childhood environment. When decisions [about the early childhood setting] are based on how children develop and learn, physically, emotionally, socially and cognitively, it is possible for each child to develop to their fullest potential within a high quality early childhood care and education environment.*

The early childhood setting, staff training and experience, opportunities for professional development for staff, and knowledge of developmentally appropriate practice all matter when it comes to whether a site is high quality or mediocre. According to the National Association for the Education of Young Children (NAEYC) position statement on Quality, Compensation, and Affordability (1995):

While good child care promotes children's development and learning, poor quality child care places children at risk. The quality of child care is directly related to children's social development and cognitive development, with better quality care associated with better outcomes regardless of child background.

Whether children are placed in family child care or a child care center, the best outcomes for children's development are linked to smaller groups, higher staff-to-child ratios, and well-trained caregivers. In addition, stability of the caregiver is an important factor in child outcomes. According to Phillips (1987):

Research on infant and toddler care suggests that very young children differentiate between stable and nonstable caregivers. Rubenstein and Howes (Quality in Child Care Study, 1997) found that twice as much interaction took place in center care between infants and head teachers as between infants and less stable volunteers. Cummings (Quality in Childcare Study, 1980) observed...infants were less resistant to transference from their mother to a stable caregiver and exhibited more positive affect when the mother left, as compared to infants who were transferred to nonstable caregivers. (p. 10)

Stable staff/child relationships are an indicator of quality early childhood programming; the responsive relationship between a child and his primary caregiver is also a critical factor in the child's social and emotional well-being, both early in life and later on as a child establishes new relationships with others.

Naomi hung on tightly to her dad while she eyed the children playing around her. Miss Rena came over and said, "There are cookies baking in the kitchen where Jackie is mommy and Abi is daddy. Do you want to play too?" Naomi hung on for a few more seconds, then got down and went over to the kitchen area. She looked back as her dad blew her a kiss and then she took out a beater and pretend eggs.

Children Need Responsive Relationships

Among the key features of an emotionally healthy environment for young children are consistency and responsiveness. We know that children grow and thrive when they have close and dependable relationships that provide love and nurturance, security, and responsive interactions (Joseph and Strain, 2004). Child developmentalists refer to this as responsive relationships. To ensure emotional health, young children must be in strong, nurturing relationships with their primary caregivers. Children spend a great deal of time today in child-care programs. If they are in programs where the caregivers take time to build, with intentionality, a trusting relationship with each child, the benefits to the child are enormous. Foremost, he will feel safe. A safe place gives a child opportunity to explore and express his emotions, helping him scaffold his developmental gains to more complex interchanges. For example, a toddler who is securely attached to her caregiver will be more apt to try new activities with new peers. New friendships bring more occasions for building new communication skills. According to one study, "children cue in on the presence of meaningful and caring adults, they attend differentially and selectively to what adults say and do, and they seek out ways to ensure even more positive attention from adults" (Joseph and Strain, 2004). A healthy emotional environment sets the stage for children to continue to learn and grow, with intentional guidance from caring adults.

The editor's note in a recent edition of "Zero to Three" points out that:

> *Child care is now a typical, rather than an exceptional experience for America's babies and toddlers. Some see this trend as a risk to healthy development, others as a chance for communities to support both children and families in the earliest years of life.*

What seems to make the difference between developmental risk and developmental opportunity in the context of infant-toddler child care is the quality of the child's experience. Child development professionals and parents agree on the elements of good quality - attention to health and safety, engaging and well-equipped caregiving environments, appropriate child-caregiver ratios and - most important - warm, responsive, stable relationships between children and caregivers (Parlakian and Fenichel, 2003).

Summary

It is in relationships that children learn to care about other people because they have established a connection between themselves and someone else. This connection teaches a child many important lessons: how to care about others, the importance of the feelings of others; how their own reactions to others impact the world around them. Relationships shape a child's own identity; the quality of the relationship is therefore critically important. Chapter 7 has several strategies for building strong relationships with children

Key Points

1. Emotional development fundamentally affects how a child perceives the world around him and so impacts how he will develop socially, physically, and cognitively.

2. We can nurture the emotional development of young children by our relationships, our practices, our words, and our example.

3. The functionalist approach to emotions says simply that the function of emotions is to prompt action to reach a personal goal.

4. Among the key features of an emotionally healthy environment for young children are consistency and responsiveness.

5. In a responsive environment, where a child has learned that needs are met when emotions are expressed, the child will feel secure and be able to move to other levels of emotional growth.

6. A healthy emotional environment sets the stage for children to continue to learn and grow, with intentional guidance from caring adults.

7. Emotional development involves the scaffolding of reactions, feelings, and responsiveness from others into more complex emotional growth.

8. If children are in programs where the caregivers take time to intentionally build a trusting relationship with each child, then the child is in a safe place to explore and express his emotions, helping him scaffold to more complex interchanges.

Chapter 2

How Do We Give Children a Strong Start?

Key 2: Ensure mastery of key emotional milestones.

This chapter explores the theories of emotional development and practical applications for us as early childhood practitioners working to enhance a child's mental health outcomes. Most of us understand the basic stages of physical development, when children first smile, speak, and walk. We understand that there are developmental milestones, supported by research, that indicate when most children typically are proficient in certain areas and activities and which new milestones will follow. Physical development is sequential and builds on what child developmentalists refer to as *mastery* of skills. For example, one must walk before he can run, babble before he can speak. The term mastery refers to both skill development and adeptness. It is widely recognized by early childhood experts as the process by which children gain a skill and then move on to the next level of that skill or a corresponding skill. Mastery crosses developmental domains and denotes a proficiency in physical, cognitive, social, and emotional growth.

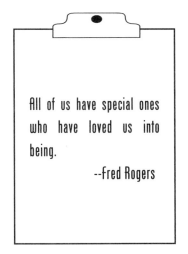

All of us have special ones who have loved us into being.

--Fred Rogers

Stages and Milestones

Emotional development also follows stages and milestones, although not as clearly in a sequential manner as physical development. Healthy emotional development depends on a child mastering foundational skills that enable him to move on to other important milestones. For instance, a child learns to trust if she's had a secure relationship with a primary caregiver; trust is needed as a foundation for a child to develop autonomy and, later, self-control. The emotional development of infants and young children is complex in many ways, involving numerous changes in the individual over time. The child and her interchanges with her environment, which may also be changing, impact core skill development. Culture, values, and family systems factor in as they influence the child and his ongoing emotional development. As young children learn to put meaning to their world, through all these influences, they follow a pathway unique to their own experiences and personality.

Makira was playing with the mommy and daddy dolls in the playhouse. She was hitting their heads together, over and over, while she used angry words. Her child-care provider came over to talk to her about what she was feeling and what was happening with the mommy and daddy. Later, as the provider talked to Makira's mom about the play, the mom confided that Makira had seen her ex-husband choke her in the garage earlier in the week.

Theoretical Models of Emotional Development

       Child developmentalists support a variety of theories on emotional development. These theories are important to understand because they offer explanations on how emotional development in young children may take place. We will look briefly at three theories in this text: the ethological model, the cognitive model, and the attachment model (Hesse, 2005). These theories will lay the foundation from which to examine stages and milestones of emotional development.

       Charles Darwin and others, such as Konrad Lorenz, espoused the *ethological model* of emotional development, believing that infants come into the world already prepared for their social and emotional roles, based on their instinct to survive. Using this theory, a child is set biologically to bond with his caregiver, which in turn promotes his chance of survival if the caregiver provides safety and security. The child's behaviors and actions are also continuously adapted in ways that help ensure a child's survival. In this model, applied to emotional development, all children come integrally equipped with the same assortment of six to ten emotions that will be present during the first two years of life, including happiness, sadness, fear, surprise, shame, and guilt. Children learn how to use these emotions from their social context; they learn which ones other people prefer and which are less desirable. Their emotional 'bank' of feelings is filled by the social experiences they have at an early age and is then adapted to fit their social environment. Since ethologists believe that emotional behaviors are understood in the perspective of their adaptability, their interest is in the whole context of a child including the influences on this adaptability from culture, biology, environment, family system, etc. Hence, in this model, *emotional development results from a child's interactions in a social context using his innate emotional cache.* Mental health is closely tied to the social environment and the child's interactions, positive and negative, to that environment.

While the ethological model says that emotional development is both instinctual and adaptable, the *cognitive model* of Jean Piaget assumes all emotional development is dependent on children's cognitive development (Hesse, 2005). In this view, a child can only understand emotions to the degree of their thinking and reasoning level; cognitive development informs emotional development. So, the more a child learns intellectually, the more sophisticated his range of emotions can become. For example, infants first experience emotions as reflexes; as they grow, they add more advanced emotions to their repertoire, like frustration or happiness. Piaget also believed that young children could not conceive of more than one emotion occurring at the same time. So, a young child would not be able to articulate feelings of sadness and joy in the same situation. In this model, it is well into school age before children can understand (1) complex emotions, (2) the occurrence of two emotions happening at the same time, and (3) their own ability to control their emotions.

Thus, as a child matures in their cognition or learning, their emotional development would follow suit. A preschooler will struggle with any complexity in emotional actions because they are not at an intellectual level that would allow them to understand it. *So, the cognitive model in emotional development says that a child's emotional development corresponds to their cognitive development.* Here, mental health is tied to intellectual proficiency.

The third major emotional development theory is the *attachment model* of Ainsworth (1965), Bowlby, and others. In this model, infants begin their emotional growth through their dependence on a secure relationship with their primary caregiver, seen as attachment. Bowlby believed that the infant was born with pre-set behaviors that would ensure a caregiver would stay near him, thus increasing the infant's chance of survival. The infant then begins to develop trust as an early emotion primarily as a result of the responsiveness of their caregiving. From here, the child can move on to explore because they have experienced security from their attachment to a primary caregiver. The child continues to benefit by learning new emotions from the vantage point of a safe haven. Conversely, a child who does not come to expect responsiveness or safety from their primary caregiver will have deficits in their acquisition of early emotions. The relationship with the primary caregiver becomes the model for all future social relationships with others. In the attachment model of emotional development, what *a child has experienced in attachments to a primary caregiver becomes what he is emotionally and what he expects from other social relationships.* Mental health is related to secure, responsive relationships.

These theories are important to early childhood practitioners because they help us derive an understanding of the origin and complexity of human emotions and how they relate to overall mental health. What is our role in supporting and sustaining strong growth? Emotional development happens in stages with the mastery of fundamental milestones that build to greater proficiency. Our knowledge of the stages and milestones of emotional development serves as a mechanism to enhance positive growth in young children.

Emotional Framework

Developmental stages and milestones comprise a strong mental health framework for young children. Some milestones are important to the development of greater skills and movement onto new stages. We will examine key milestones and their application to emotional development in this chapter. Important emotional objectives for children, according to research from the Mayo Clinic, include secure attachment relationships, trust-building, and self-concept. A newborn to three month old, for example, should be able to distinguish his primary caregiver by scent and, by two months old, be able to discriminate among different voices and tastes. This ability to make distinctions helps the child build attachment to his primary caregiver and scaffold that security attachment to a beginning exploration of his social world. Also at this age, a child will learn that objects disappear and reappear quickly, which becomes important as a foundation for the child's later development of trust. At six to nine months, a child will participate in imitation games, begin to understand that an object out of sight may be concealed behind something else, and will begin to know his name, further strengthening the attachment relationship and moving him toward self-awareness. By 12 to 18 months, a young child will start to see that some words are symbols for objects, will have an increased attention span, will imitate activities, and remember past events for longer periods. This is foundational as well to affiliation, trust, and later social relationships. Child developmentalists are familiar with milestones or skill acquisitions that signal a proficiency in a measurable ability. Proficiencies cluster into *stages,* which make up healthy development (Kaufman, 2005). Next we will examine different views on the stages of emotional development in young children.

Seth, age 4, is showing his little brother and caregiver his new magic trick. He puts a building block on his shoulder and says the magic words as he tucks the building block in his shirt. The caregiver claps enthusiastically as Seth laughs with delight.

Some child developmentalists such as Warhol and Emde describe emotional development as a series of *transitions* as children age, rather than mastered milestones which scaffold to other skill development (Croft and Hewitt, 2004). Seeing development as a series of transitions means that emotional growth is a result of the "periods of reorganization" which a child goes through in their physical and cognitive development. So, as he ages, a child moves from social smiling and focused attachment to self-reflective awareness and acquisition of other emotions like shame and empathy. Emde's (Croft and Hewitt, 2004) emotional development model follows these seven transitions:

1. Birth: crying, interest/attentiveness, capacities for self-soothing.

2. Two to three months: onset of social smile, eye-to-eye social contact, awakening of sociability.

3. Five-months: focused attachment, infant distress on approach of stranger, distress upon separation from primary caregivers, shared meaning in games like peek-a-boo.

4. Ten to 13 months: marked by onset of walking and its socio-emotional consequences, as in distress at caregiver prohibitions; uses emotions to communicate a sense of pride.

5. Eighteen to 22 months: earmarked as transitions from infancy to early childhood because the changes are major. Beginning of self-reflective awareness, multi-word speech, moral emotions (expectations of what is right and distress at violations), empathy, shame expressions.

6. Three to four years: Ability to use language to share experiences with others, regulation of emotions, greater understanding of family relationships.

7. Five to seven years: Marked by enhanced cognitive, perceptual, and attentional capacities for social emotional regulation.

Support for Essential Building Blocks

At each of these transition points we must consider the individual child, their environment, family system, culture, ability and what influences they will have at each of the intervals. For example, how the family addresses misconduct influences expression of shame at 18 to 22 months. Some families see the breaking of their rules as misbehavior and teach a child that mistakes are part of learning, so shame will be less reinforced. Culture plays a large influence in these transitions as well. A culture that supports more interdependency in children than independence will influence the degree to which empathy is established. Children begin at infancy with core abilities, such as signaling distress with a cry, which are built on to greater, more refined skills such as regulation of emotions, and the progression and level of mastery depends on the responsive nature of care for each child as well as the child's natural abilities and reinforcements. The young child starts with essential building blocks and the early childhood practitioner influences the ultimate child outcomes for positive mental health.

Greenspan's Four Stages

Dr. Stanley Greenspan (1997), a leading early childhood expert, describes the process of acquiring developmental skills differently than Emde's periods of transitions. According to Greenspan, there are four main stages which help a child learn to think and grow emotionally. He has organized the emotional development of a child into the following areas:

1). *Engagement:* This stage occurs in the first eight months of life, when children learn to attend and engage by looking into a caregiver's eyes, focusing on the voice of the caregiver, paying attention to the world around them. Not only do infants learn to share attention with a caregiver, they also learn by 3 or 4 months that interactions can be pleasurable. They learn positive emotions. A baby may smile, or make vocalizations along with their caregiver. In the absence of a trusting, positive experience, an infant can learn distrust, suspiciousness, or apathy—not a good foundation for later learning. However, in a responsive relationship, an infant can learn that their emotions can impact their world in a positive way, helping them to move into the next stage of emotional development.

2). *Two-Way Communication:* Developing a capacity for two-way communication is the second emotional stage that children need to master. Two-way communication means they learn to signal their own needs and intentions and seek to understand someone else's needs. It becomes an interaction. This is usually achieved around 6-18 months. At around 18 months, children begin stringing together "circles of communication" that are part of their relationship with the caregivers around them. In a circle of communication, the child approaches a caregiver, the caregiver responds back, and the child moves on, opening and closing the circle. Two-way communication is the basis for later proficiency in language acquisition. It is also where other important learning occurs about relationships and interactions, helping a child make sense of her world. The impact here lies in the give and take between a child and the important people in her life; if caregiving is responsive to the child, she learns that she is important to someone, that her feelings and needs matter. If two-way communication seldom occurs, the child learns her needs may not be met or that she is not valued. This is a critically important stage for a child's later development of self-esteem, a key component of strong mental health.

3). *Shared Meaning*: Learning shared meaning comes around the ages of 18-36 months, as children begin to see how their behaviors, sensations, and gestures relate to the world of ideas. This is evident in language when a child says, "I am happy." He is using an idea, with words, to communicate a feeling. Pretend play is a key component in developing shared meaning. With pretend play, children experiment with words and actions. Also, this is the stage where children begin to master complex concepts like "up and down" or "hot and cold." It is also at the shared meaning stage that children begin to understand on a symbolic level; for instance, understanding word or number concepts, or enjoying a story. Shared meaning is important to a child's emotional development because it forms the basis for effective communication and the understanding of one's own nature and feelings and how they relate to the rest of the world.

4). *Emotional Thinking:* In this stage, children who are 3-5 years old are organizing ideas of experiences and learning how to connect different ideas. A sense of "self" and a sense of "others" and the interactions between both begin to take hold. Children can now see themselves in space and time. As they begin to understand space and time, they can learn to control impulses: "If I take my nap, then I can ride my bike after I wake up." Children begin to organize different emotions with an understanding of space and time: "I am in school now, Mommy is at home, and I'll see her after lunch." This is a key stage for children to learn what is healthy or acceptable in their emotions and how to control them. In Chapter 4 we will discuss in depth how a child develops self-regulation and the importance of it In emotional thinking a child is learning, for example, that aggression is not the most constructive way to get something he wants. They are beginning to learn socially acceptable ways to negotiate differences and compromise. Rates of aggression in young children show that aggression tends to peak around age 3 and begins to decline, indicating children are learning the finer arts of sharing and friendship. Emotional thinking is important to a child's social relationships and secure mental health.

Five-week-old Jake started crying when his mom put him down in the infant seat. She let him cry for a minute or so, until she saw he wasn't consoling himself. She reached down and picked him up again. He cried for another minute and then relaxed in her hold. He made some hiccup sounds and fell back asleep.

Emotional Development as Acquired Skills

Greenspan's work, like Emde's, points to the importance of recognizing how different children are at the various infant-to-preschool ages and how much their emotional development is interrelated to their environment, their caregiving, and their own unique personalities. Gehrke (cited in Croft and Hewitt, 2004) looks at emotional development in another way. Through the work of Dr. Bruce Perry (2000), he identifies it as a series of acquired skills. Gehrke explains that following Perry's model, a child must develop the following emotional and social skills in order, though each child will move through at her own rate. These skills–attachment, self-regulation, affiliation, awareness, tolerance, and respect–defined as:

1. Attachment - the capacity to form and maintain relationships. At the foundation of the creation of a healthy child.
2. Self-Regulation - the ability to read and respond to internal states appropriately. If children are unable to recognize what's going on inside them, getting along with others and regulating behavior is difficult.
3. Affiliation - the ability to join with others and contribute to a group. If children haven't developed self-regulation, they will have difficulty with affiliation.
4. Awareness - the capacity to recognize the needs, interests, strengths, and value in others. Young children tend to group others very simply and with sameness, which interferes with seeing people as they really are. Children must be with people who are different. Children must have a chance to be with the elderly and children of other ages, too.

5. Tolerance - a child's capacity to understand and accept how others are different from themselves.

6. Respect - the capacity to value the variety of gifts and capacities of others and in yourself. This concept is the most difficult. If children can't accept their own shortcomings, self-respect becomes difficult, causing them to focus on the shortcomings of others in a negative way. When we raise our children with "don't do this, don't do that," the brain spends much more time focusing on shortcomings instead of strengths. It is important to help children develop in a positive way (Gehrke, 2004).

Perry's six acquired skills model relates well to the work of Emde and Greenspan because all three contain important components that must be present and supported by caregivers in order to ensure healthy and secure emotional development. The outcomes of these models can be integrated into our relationships with children whether we regard emotional proficiencies as a series of stages, transitions, or acquired skills.

Each of these child development experts articulate in a similar manner the progression that children go through as the child's emotional person is developed. These progressions contain the same essential elements: building of trust through responsive caregiving, developing an understanding of person and the relationship of self to others, as well as more sophisticated mental health goals such as regulation, empathy, and caring for others outside of self. These skills do not come automatically or instinctively; they are taught and reinforced by the significant caregivers in a child's life. Next to a parent, the early childhood caregiver is perhaps the most significant nurturer of a child through these critical early stages.

As children progress emotionally in stages, much the way they develop physically, skills they have already achieved are embedded into new proficiencies as they reach the next stage. Many experts in the field believe that in the first 4 to 5 years of life, children learn critical ideas about life through their relationships with others. In these relationships, basic emotional stages are mastered (or not), and set the stage for cognitive learning. To ensure that later learning is successful, it is important to make sure early emotional learning takes place in a positive and nurturing environment.

Key 2: Ensure mastery of emotional milestones

Experts agree that for optimal development, certain important characteristics must be met in different ages and stages. According to the National Center on Birth Defects and Developmental Disabilities, the following are key emotional milestones for young children at various developmental ages:

3 months:
- Begins to develop a social smile
- Enjoys playing with other people and may cry when playing stops
- Becomes more expressive and communicates more with face and body
- Imitates some movements and facial expressions

7 months:
- Enjoys social play
- Interested in mirror images
- Responds to other people's expressions of emotion and often appears joyful

By end of 1 year:

- Shy or anxious with strangers

- Cries when mother or father leaves

- Enjoys imitating people in his play

- Shows specific preferences for certain people and toys

- Tests parental responses to his actions during feedings

- Tests parental responses to his behavior

- May be fearful in some situations

- Prefers mother and/or regular caregiver over all others

- Repeats sounds or gestures for attention

By end of 2 years:

- Imitates behavior of others, especially adults and older children

- More aware of herself as separate from others

- More excited about company of other children

- Demonstrates increasing independence

- Begins to show defiant behavior

- Separation anxiety increases toward midyear then fades

By end of 3 years:

- Imitates adults and playmates

- Spontaneously shows affection for familiar playmates

- Can take turns in games

- Understands concept of "mine" and "his/hers"

- Expresses affection openly

- Expresses a wide range of emotions

- Separates easily from parents

- Objects to major changes in routine

By end of 4 years:

- Interested in new experiences

- Cooperates with other children

- Plays "Mom" or "Dad"

- Increasingly inventive in fantasy play

- Negotiates solutions to conflicts

- More independent

- Imagines that many unfamiliar images may be "monsters"

- Views self as a whole person involving body, mind, and feelings

- Often cannot tell the difference between fantasy and reality

By end of 5 years:

- Wants to please friends

- Wants to be like her friends

- More likely to agree to rules

- Shows more independence and may even visit a next-door neighbor by herself

- Aware of gender

- Able to distinguish fantasy from reality

- Sometimes demanding, sometimes eagerly cooperative

In your work as an early childhood educator and caregiver, you will encounter children at different mastery levels of the emotional milestones necessary for their development. What can you as an early childhood practitioner do to enhance a child's mental health? One of the key roles you play is in providing responsive caregiving. Research has linked responsive caregiving to many positive outcomes for children. For many caregivers it seems intuitive to respond to children's needs, but in fact, intentionality in responsiveness can greatly enhance the child's relationship with their caregiver and their healthy emotional development. If we meet a child's needs, they will feel more secure in their world, which encourages exploration and social navigating. Children who are frequently ignored or neglected learn that their needs are not important, that the world is not a safe place, and that emotions are negative. This sets up a framework of harm to their mental health.

Another effective strategy for early childhood professionals, according to Wittmer and Honig (1994), is to encourage how children understand their own feelings and the feelings of others through our interactions and our program activities. We can teach children to express themselves with words, to put their emotions into words, and to understand what their feelings mean. Caregivers must model the words we want children to learn, like "You look like you are sad because your mom had to leave." Research cited by Wittmer and Honig (1994) shows that children become aware of different feelings at different ages, and we must be responsive to their developmental stage. For instance, "children from ages 3 to 8 are becoming aware of *happy feelings* (3½ years) and *fear* (3½ to 4 years). As we work with young children we can intentionally use words that explain these fundamental feelings, as well as provide opportunities for children to practice these emotions with books and other print media, dramatic play, and other social activities.

Wisdom from the Field

A cohort of early childhood educators offered their ideas on teaching children how to express their feelings. The following are useful strategies for encouraging emotional expression:

- Read books about children's feelings at circle time and follow up with talking to the whole group about their reaction to the book. Ask open-ended questions about the subject of the book.

- Create "Feelings Cubes" with the children. Use Polaroid® pictures of each child or use magazine pictures. Let the children keep their cube at the center or home child care and encourage them to use them during the day. Ask questions about why they are feeling a particular way.

- Practice different feelings with dramatic play, dolls, blocks and other manipulatives. Give them words for their feelings. Help them create solutions to hard or difficult feelings, like fear, anger, or sadness. Allow them to talk through scary feelings. Give them "If I feel like this, I can do this" role plays.

- Create an atmosphere of safety and security. Help the children know it is a safe place to "have a feeling." Give them ways to show how they are feeling that won't hurt other children or themselves. Help them know it's okay to be mad, for example, and talk about some things they can do when they are mad.

- Display books, posters, and other toys that show a variety of expressions and the acting out of various feelings. Provide a broad range of dramatic play materials.

Summary

This chapter lays out the key emotional milestones for young children as they develop from birth through early childhood. Their mental health outcomes depend on successful acquisition of emotional skills and support through important stages of growth.

Key Points

1. Emotional development follows stages and milestones, although not in such a clearly sequential manner as physical development.

2. Healthy emotional development does depend on mastery of foundational pieces in order to move on to other important milestones.

3. Children begin at infancy with core abilities, such as signaling distress with a cry, which build on to greater, more refined skills such as regulation of emotions, and the progression and level of mastery depends on the responsive nature of care for each child.

4. Emotional development sets the stage for all other development, including cognitive, physical, and social growth.

5. Definitions of emotional development include stages, milestones, transitions, or acquired skills.

6. Caregivers can enhance a child's emotional development by providing responsiveness, consistency, safety, and security.

Chapter 3

Why Do Children Act the Way They Do?

Key 3: Understanding how a child is "wired."

What makes up a child's temperament?

Children come into this world "wired" a certain way, gifts from their parents and DNA. They have individual characteristics and patterns of behavior that we call their *temperament*. Temperament is what makes each child unique in how they will react to the world around them, whether we are changing their diaper or teaching them to ride a bike. The definition of temperament includes a person's behavioral style, the "how" of what they do. In other words, temperament is the "characteristic way that the individual experiences and responds to the internal and external environment" (Warhol, 1998). It is unique to each child. There is an abundance of research supporting the concept that personality differences in children are real. They each have a temperament comprised

> And that you're learning how important you are, how important each person you see can be. Discovering each one's specialty is the most important learning.
>
> --Fred Rogers

of many pieces, what experts call temperament traits. Many child developmentalists believe that a child's personality is half genetic and half environment. Their environment includes the physical and social environment, as well as the physical health of the child. So a child reflects the world around him through the person they were born as... marvelous!

This story from a family child-care provider illustrates how temperament impacts children's behaviors and interactions with others:

"I began to observe one of my child care parent's reactions to their child's behavior during drop off and pick up times. Michelle has a very strong will and is active and aggressive. She has her own agenda as far as if she wants to give her parents a kiss and hug goodbye before they leave, or when she is ready to quit playing and go to the car when her parents pick her up. They try reasoning with her, polite requests, suggestions, and distractions, to no avail. Their strategies do not match her higher intensity temperament and so they are not very successful impacting her behavior. On the other hand, Carmen is quiet and anxious, and her parents are much more successful in dealing with her behavior using reasoning, polite requests, suggestions, and distractions. Since sharing information about temperament with Michelle's parents, they have changed how they react to her behavior. They now give less energy to her intensity and they use stronger rewards for compliance. Drop off and pick up times have been less stressful on all of us."

In this child-care provider's experience, the temperament of both girls had a definite impact on their reaction to the everyday experience of drop-off and pick-up. The children reacted uniquely to their parents' actions based on their personality tendencies. This story illustrates how temperament plays an important role in the behavior of children.

The Nine Temperament Traits

Children are unique from the moment they are born. A child's inborn temperament is a key influence on a child's mental health because it fundamentally affects how a child sees his relationship to the world around him. Again, temperament is the way in which we are all "wired." Temperament influences how each person deals with the world. Certain behavior clusters seem to go with certain combinations of temperament traits. Temperament is based on nine characteristics first articulated by Thomas and Chess (1970) in their long-term study of infants and their relationship to their parents. They visited families monthly, observing an infant's behaviors when relating to his parents and when left alone. They grouped the behaviors into nine categories that they felt represented the range of individual differences they had observed. These nine temperaments still stand today:

1. Activity Level—How active is the child from an early age?
2. Distractibility—How easily is the child distracted?
3. Persistence—Does the child stay with something she likes? If he wants something, how persistent or stubborn is he?
4. Adaptability—How does the child deal with transitions or changes in routine?
5. Approach/Withdraw—What is the child's initial response to newness? What is his reaction to new foods, places, activities, people, and clothes?
6. Intensity—How loud is the child, whether happy or unhappy?
7. Regularity—How predictable is the child in her patterns of sleep, appetite, or bodily functions?
8. Sensory Threshold—How does the child react to sensory stimulation: noise, light, colors, smells, pain, tastes, textures in clothing and food? Is she over-stimulated or bothered by different sensations?
9. Mood—What is the child's predominant mood? Is he more negative or positive generally?

The work of Thomas and Chess has been validated over the last 50 years. Very young children are developing in many areas including physically, socially, cognitively, and emotionally, and these areas of development are closely related. Factoring in the temperament traits of an infant or young child, helps caregivers better meet each child's individual developing needs.

A **tenth temperament trait** was added in recent years to address a child's emotional sensitivity. It is defined as the ease or difficulty with which a child responds emotionally to a situation. This trait has two sub-scales, one for sensitivity to one's own feelings and one for sensitivity to others' feelings.

Two-year-old Althea stacks several blocks, one on top of another, until they become unbalanced and fall over. She begins to build again, in the same fashion, one on top of another, until they crash down again. She repeats this process over and over, until she tires of blocks and begins to look for her sippy cup.

Key 3: Understand how a child is "wired."

As we focus on how mental health in young children emerges, we can learn much about how to enhance that development if we understand a child's core temperament. Temperament is key to how a child will react to his world and often how the world will react to the child. Stanley Turecki (2000), in his book *The Difficult Child*, describes how each of the temperament traits, in their extremes of high or low, relates specifically to infant behaviors:

High Activity Level:
An extremely fussy, squirmy or vigorous baby.

Poor Adaptability:
Reacts badly to changes in the routine.

Initial/Withdrawl:
Protests, fusses when first introduced to new foods, new places, or new people.

High Intensity:
Screams in distress or delight, a "loud" baby.

Irregularity:
Feeding and sleeping are very hard to schedule, an "unpredictable" baby.

Low Sensory Threshold:
Easily bothered by noises, lights, and texture of clothes, a sensitive, "jumpy" baby.

Negative Mood:
Fusses, whimpers, or cries a great deal, an "unhappy" baby.

Looking at the list of infant reactions above, we can see it is a small leap from a child's temperament to their behaviors and the reactions of others to them, and to their healthy or unhealthy emotional development. For instance, if an infant has poor adaptability and reacts with negativity to changes in routine, and the child care providers of that infant change frequently over a period of months, emotionally the baby is going to be spending a lot of energy in fear, anger, and anxiety, building towards a hyper state of arousal at times. One infant with a more relaxed temperament toward changes might be growing within Greenspan's two-way communication stage, while a distressed infant is still struggling with basic trust. The distressed infant is not learning that his world is a safe place where he can explore and invest in the reactions of others. Rather, he is going to stay self-focused and look inward. He is not in a setting where he can thrive emotionally. This early response from the environment to the child's temperament can have a lasting impact on the infant's mental health.

Why Does Understanding Temperament Matter?

Understanding the role of temperament in a child's emotional development is key to understanding "who" the child is—their behaviors, learning needs and styles, social skills and abilities, how they react to the world around them—and what they need from us. If we see temperament as a core quality of the person the child is, and also understand environmental impacts as variables we have some control over, we can stage the most effective environment for each child. Thomas and Chess (1970) called this process "goodness of fit" to describe how temperament and environment can work together toward favorable outcomes for children. If we ignore temperament, we lose out on vital information about who the child is and how they will react to our setting and practices. If we try to deny or work against the child's basic temperament characteristics, we set the stage for conflict between the child and ourselves, and increase stress for both of us. For instance, if a child's core temperament trait is strong on irregularity, the child's caregiver will be increasingly frustrated if she insists on feeding each day at the same time, or insisting on naps at the same time each day for all children. If a child is high in their regularity, he will have problems when the routine is varied or the schedule is ambiguous. We create the goodness of fit by knowing each child's temperament and making adaptations throughout the day. If a child needs routine, we provide daily picture schedules and visual or auditory warnings if the routine is changing. For the child with low regularity, we provide adjustments like a quiet area for resting when he tires, or snacks throughout the day. As children grow older they will learn to moderate themselves more, but we have to help them get to this point by slowly increasing patterns and rhythms while also acknowledging the differences. So, a child will be encouraged to eat at snack time, but he will have the option for a munchie at a different time of the day. This involves flexibility on the part of the educator, but the long-term gain for the provider is a positive payoff in the child's emotional reactions and behaviors.

Wisdom from the Field

An early childhood teacher writes, "If a child is always made to feel that their behaviors are wrong (i.e., a child with high impulsivity who often acts before giving it a lot of thought) then the child will begin to see his whole self as 'wrong' and this will adversely affect his self concept. But if someone honors his temperament and works on his strengths, then the child will see that he is worthy and will want to learn more."

Strategies for Working with Different Temperaments

The following are some basic strategies for working with each of the ten temperament traits in young children. "Low" and "high" are descriptors of the degree of the temperament manifested in the child's actions, demeanor, and responses to the world around him. A high activity level, for example, would indicate a child who moves a lot, compared with a child with low activity level who seems to have minimum energy. Embedding these strategies into everyday practice will help ensure that the early childhood setting is a safe and nurturing place for all children to grow and develop in a healthy manner, regardless of temperament traits.

1. Activity Level: An overall preference for active or inactive play; and overall energy level throughout the day.

Low Activity:
- Slowly introduce new, more active pastimes, being careful to watch the child for cues of over-stimulation.
- Provide calm pastimes/activities that are enjoyable and developmentally appropriate.
- Observe carefully for interest in areas that could be built into new, more active opportunities.
- Watch your language usage that might indicate judgment around low activity in children. For example, avoid saying things like, "He's not interested in anything" or, "She's so quiet you forget she's there."

High Activity:
- Allow time for large muscle exercise.
- Give child gentle touches to remind to slow down, relax.
- Provide interesting and challenging calm activities. Watch for child's cues and gradually increase the time for calm activities.
- Provide equipment that is well-constructed and sturdy for active play.
- Provide clear rules and limits on how much activity you allow at certain times and places.
- Provide safe environments and evaluate risks.
- Watch your language usage that might indicate judgment around high activity in children. For example, avoid saying things like, "He's so hyperactive he must have A.D.H.D." or, "She's not going to set the world on fire, is she?"

2. Regularity: The day-to-day predictability of hunger, sleep, and elimination.

Low Regularity:
- Be aware that the child is responding to his own body needs, not trying to irritate the practitioner or be disruptive.

- Encourage regularity where it is appropriate; have schedules that are reliable and set patterns for children.

- Create cues that will help the child adapt to the schedule so he can begin to anticipate regular times for eating, etc.

- Help the child to develop skills of self-regulation. For example, have snacks available for the child to access between regular meal times.

- Help the child learn to read his own body cues. Give a child words for hungry, tired, etc.

- Look for any regularity in the child and help him recognize and build on it.

- Recognize that some children will not be very regular in their eating, sleeping, or elimination needs. Make sure there are accommodations in place for children who are not regular in their body functions.

3. Adaptability: How easily a child adjusts to attempts to influence or change what she is doing or thinking.

Low Adaptability:
- Be aware of transitions and keep them to a minimum.

- Develop cues for the child prior to a transition to give him time to get ready for the change.

- Help the child express with words his feelings about changing an activity.

- If a change in schedule is expected, prepare the child as much as possible beforehand. If a change comes unexpectedly, be aware of the changes in the child's reactions, behaviors, etc. Anticipate an increased stress level in the child.

- Keep a consistent schedule each day and keep changes to a minimum.

- Tools such as schedule boards are effective in helping a child with low adaptability prepare for the next change or transition.

4. Approach/Withdrawn: A child's initial tendency for responding to a new experience, a new person, or a new environment.

Quick to Approach:

- Be aware of a child's tendency to embrace new people or experiences and supervise appropriately.

- Continually check the environment for health and safety concerns.

- Be accepting of a child's messiness; help children develop better skills finishing or cleaning up a project.

- Look for ways to help a child develop self-regulation skills

Slow to approach/ Withdrawn:

- Give children ample time to adjust to a new person, place, etc.

- Be aware of staff changes and try to keep to a minimum.

- Introduce changes slowly, but do introduce new things to the child. Help him learn to express with words his feelings about new foods, toys, etc.

5. Intensity: The amount of energy a child commonly uses to express emotions.

High Intensity:

- Help the child become more aware of his reactions. Help him learn to read his own cues.

- Help the child learn to use words to express his feelings. Help him use words to ask for help when he is feeling "out of control."

- Provide activities that are calming; help the child learn to use quiet activities to self regulate.

- If a child becomes upset, look for imaginative ways to calm him, like pretending he is dressing up for a special dance.

- Teach the child how and where to take a break. Provide a place for down time.

- Provide opportunities for a child to 'use' his high intensity, i.e., dramatic play. Be a good audience to his performances.

- Be aware that a child with high intensity will be louder sometimes. Celebrate the value of great exuberance.

6. Distractibility: How easily things going on around a child interrupt thought processes or attention.

High Distractibility:

- Be aware of sensory stimulation in the early childhood environment. Try to keep it to a minimum when possible.

- Provide space for quiet time with few distractions.

- Give fewer choices.

- Use many sensory approaches to communicate with the child; help him get your message through several different mediums. For example, touch his arm while you are speaking, or use a touch to the shoulder to help him refocus.

- Use good eye contact when relaying a message to a child. Try to minimize other distractions when you are giving instructions or information.

- Break directions into several parts and give one part at a time. Give positive reinforcement to a child for completing each part.

- Help the child learn his body cues; help him develop tools for self-regulation. Ask what works for him.

- Be aware of language and say what is expected from the child; be clear in expectations.

- Try to avoid interruptions when giving directions, instructions, and information.

- Help children feel good about what they can do; avoid judgments about what they don't do.

7. **Mood:** The amount of pleasant, joyful and friendly behavior as contrasted with unpleasant, crying, and unfriendly behavior.

Negative Mood:

- Increase pleasant interactions for the child within the early childhood environment, through books, music, etc.

- Be sensitive to sensory stimulation and how it may impact the mood of the child. If a particular sensory stimulation increases a child's positive mood, look for more ways to incorporate it into the program, like soft music or scents.

- Incorporate into the regular schedule, activities that are pleasant for the child.

- Watch for signs of depression and make an appropriate referral for a child who is persistently sad, eats and sleeps poorly, and shows other signs of depression.

- Recognize mood as part of who the child is, and avoid taking his reactions personally. Avoid using judgmental language about the child to him or to staff.

- Encourage the child to develop self-expression skills. Model positive language for the child to use.

8. Persistence: The length of time a child will continue to make an effort, especially when the task gets hard.

Low Persistence:

- Be aware of triggers that may discourage a child from finishing a task.

- Offer different options for completing an activity; vary the options whenever possible to generate interest. For example, at clean up, ask the child to pick up the blue Legos® instead of all the Legos® while you help him.

- Be aware of sensory stimulation that may interfere with a child's ability to stay on task; lessen environmental distractions when possible.

- Build on what engages the child; create opportunities for the child to delve more deeply into interest areas.

- Positively reinforce a child for staying with a task. Stretch out the time between reinforcers to increase a child's persistence. Build on the child's sense of success in completing an activity, job, game, etc.

High Persistence:

- Be aware of and avoid power struggles with a child. Diffuse a situation as quickly as possible that might escalate into a power struggle. For example, a child who does not like to leave an activity may need several warnings; discuss the warnings ahead of time with the child so he knows what to expect.

- Recognize that the practitioner and the child both have a "position" to defend - model to the child looking for solutions instead of "winning."

- Help the child learn to use his words to express his needs or wants rather than hitting, pushing, etc.

- Include the child in brainstorming for solutions to a conflict.

- Have clear rules and clear expectations; be consistent with consequences.

- Introduce variations to an activity that might stimulate the child to try something new.

- Value the child's persistence; help him find ways to use this temperament trait in positive ways.

9. **Sensory Awareness:** How sensitive a child is in each of her sensory channels: pain, touch, taste, smell, hearing and sight.

High Sensory Awareness:

- Look for sensory triggers, i.e., tags in clothes, sock seams, bright lights, sounds, smells.

- Check stimulation levels; reduce where possible.

- Provide a place in which a child with high sensory needs can retreat, if necessary.

- Help a child learn his own body cues for over-stimulation.

- Be aware of the early childhood environment for sensory overload, including temperature, noise level, clutter on walls, etc. Give the child the opportunity to change the environment herself when possible.

- Help the child use words to describe how she is feeling.

Low Sensory Awareness:

- Help increase sensory awareness by introducing new tastes, sounds, etc. through art, music, cooking, etc.

- Teach children to be aware of their own bodies, e.g., "Is your engine low, high, or just right?"

- Reinforce a child's exploration of new sensations.

- Be alert to health and safety issues for a child who may not be aware of his senses.

10. Emotional Sensitivity: The ease or difficulty with which the child responds emotionally to a situation. This trait has two sub-scales, one for sensitivity to one's own feelings and one for sensitivity to others' feelings.

Oversensitive:

- Help children find words to express their feelings about themselves and about others.

- Validate feelings!

- Be aware of videos, etc., that may frighten or overwhelm the child.

- Give the child time and space to regulate his own emotions.

- Be aware of a child's "overload" signals; have cues for the child to help him check his emotions.

Undersensitive:

- Work with the child on expressing his feelings in words, being more aware of others around them.

- Use videos, books, etc., to model the portrayal of emotions in positive ways. Find ways to teach a child about his feelings and the feelings of others.

- Use positive reinforcers when a child shows sensitivity to someone else. Tell the child why that was a positive interaction.

- Celebrate even small victories with the child!
  (Croft and Hewitt, 2004).

Sara looked at her caregiver with a solemn face, even as the provider made funny faces trying to make her laugh. Ever so slightly, she turned up the corners of her mouth, not with laughter but with acknowledgment of the provider's efforts in trying to entertain her.

Summary

As early childhood educators and professionals, we have the ability to make the most out of each child's temperament and personality through sensitivity, awareness, and knowledge of developmentally appropriate practice. Some temperament traits are more challenging than others, but seeing each child as a whole person, not just one temperament trait, will help us appreciate the unique gifts each child brings to our programs. A child's mental health depends on caregivers who enhance natural temperament traits into healthy behaviors that promote emotional and social growth.

Key Points

1. All children have individual characteristics and patterns of behavior that are called temperaments.

2. Temperaments are comprised of ten distinct traits and play an important role in the behavior of all children.

3. Temperament is key to how a child will react to his world and often how the world will react to the child.

4. This early response from the environment to the child's temperament can have a lasting impact on the infant's mental health.

5. Flexibility on the part of the educator can result in a positive payoff in a child's behavior.

6. Embedding strategies into everyday practice will help ensure that the early childhood setting is a safe and nurturing place for all children to grow and develop in a healthy manner, regardless of temperament traits.

7. As early childhood educators and professionals, we have the ability to make the most out of each child's temperament and personality through sensitivity, awareness, and knowledge of developmentally appropriate practice.

Chapter 4

How to Teach Children to Know Their Own Engines

Key 4: Teach self-regulation skills.

What is Emotional Regulation?

An important emotional achievement for children in early childhood, one that is crucial to their positive mental health, is the ability to regulate with consistency their own emotions and feelings. Perhaps the mastery of no other single milestone will have greater impact on a child and her relationships with others for the rest of her life. In fact, positive mental health may depend on it. So what is meant by emotional regulation? Katz (1997) explains it as:

> Let's think of something to do while we're waiting
> While we're waiting for something new to do.
> Let's try to think up a song while we're waiting
> That's liberating and will be true to you.
>
> --Fred Rogers

> *The ability to respond to the ongoing demands of experience (Jamal takes Christopher's Elmo® doll) with the range of emotions in a manner that is socially tolerable (Christopher begins to cry loudly) and sufficiently flexible to permit spontaneous reactions as well as the ability to delay spontaneous reactions as needed (teacher gives another Elmo® doll to Christopher who returns to play after soothing self). Emotions form the underlying bases for motivation, provoke problem-solving, and stimulate participation in a wide variety of activities and situations.*

61

Emotions are essential adaptive capacities that contribute to survival. (p. 3)

For children, the ability to regulate their emotional reactions is a key component to healthy emotional development. First, it enables them to make and keep friends—*as two children work together to build a tower in the block area, one child accidentally knocks over the structure as he reaches for another block. His friend is immediately upset by the collapse, but controls his reaction to hit his fellow builder with a stray piece. Instead, he growls to himself and proceeds to begin the process of rebuilding.* This is not an accidental response by the child whose play has been disrupted by his friend—it is a response that has been nurtured by his relationship with his caregiver and her understanding of his own unique temperament needs. Children are taught, or not taught, emotional regulation through their interactions with caregivers, peers, family, and other community members. They will learn to react from what has been modeled to them and those reactions will be reinforced by what 'works' for them in achieving their personal goals.

Second, emotional regulation helps a child build a positive self-view. As a young child learns that she can control her feelings and her impulses, she is empowered by that knowledge. She begins to see herself as successful, as competent. She can navigate a social interaction with a positive outcome. Positive reinforcement by a primary caregiver will make her more apt to repeat her successful behavior of self-regulation. This point cannot be made too strongly—a child who knows he can control his reactions is a child who will be comfortable in his role in the world around him. **The development of self-regulation is a cornerstone of strong mental health**. As a child develops their own sense of self-regulatory responses to feelings and situations, it will begin to permeate to all areas of their behavior.

Alexandro was at the art table with Alena, painting with food-coloring water in paper cups. Alena poured all the cups into one cup, turning it brown. Alexandro said, "Alena, NO!" Alena looked regretfully at the dark color and said to her friend, "I don't want to paint with brown."

The Role of Support in Infancy

Research has shown that emotional regulation begins early, in infancy. Babies begin to regulate their emotions through what Bromwich (1997) calls "interactive experience." A baby learns from his parents or primary caregiver what reaction to expect to his cries, coos, or smiles. Is he given a soft blanket or a pacifier; does he hear a gentle hum? All these positive actions help to support the infant's mechanism for self-regulation. He then transfers what he has learned to the other caregivers in his young life. He learns what he can expect as a response to his emotional actions (the cry, coo, or smile). This expectation can be trusting, or mistrusting, depending on his early experiences. Why is this important? It cannot be emphasized enough that emotional regulation is a skill that is necessary for humans to be successful in their relationships with one another. We have, from the time children are born, to teach them these regulation skills. Bromwich further describes this interactive process:

> *Once the infant has developed trust—a secure attachment to the parent—several things are likely to happen. The infant uses the adult as a secure base from which he can distance himself and explore his human and physical environment. On the other hand, an infant who experiences more distrust than trust may not develop a secure attachment to an adult caregiver. For example, an infant gets no*

response to crying, smiling, or vocalizing over a period of several weeks. He gradually learns not to anticipate responses to his signals and therefore stops trying to communicate. The infant tends to become passive—and no longer expresses his needs and wants. The result is a passive baby, unmotivated to communicate or make contact with any part of his world. This lack of motivation impedes development in all areas because the infant ceases to pay much attention to anything in the environment. (p. 12-13)

As we look at the keys to promoting children's mental health, it is clear that a child who is nurtured by a responsive caregiver early on will begin to learn from those experiences, the self-regulation skills which he will later apply to more complex emotional situations. A child, on the other hand, whose emotional needs have been neglected or infrequently responded to with positive caregiving, will be disadvantaged as he develops his coping mechanisms for emotional reactions. The foundation of support for the child's healthy emotional self-regulation is missing. Without that foundation, a child is going to struggle to control his feelings, which will then impact his relationship to peers and to other caregivers.

Four-year-old Allysa has been meticulously gluing leaves, sticks and other nature objects onto a piece of paper in a heart design. As she finishes the project, she picks it up to move it to another table to dry. In the moving, a corner of the paper drops and several pieces fall off. Allysa cries: "It's ruined, now it's ugly. I hate it." She drops the entire piece onto the floor, frustrated and angry.

As children move from infancy into toddlerhood and preschool age, they begin to experience other emotions more complex than an infant's cry for comfort. They become part of a complicated social world where, early on, they need to learn to successfully function within a myriad of emotions that invoke sometimes strong reactions: fear, anger, frustration. If their foundation has been secure and trusting, they will have emotional building blocks that will help them scaffold their self-regulatory skills to new situations. Katz (1997) emphasizes:

> *The progression from relying on parents for regulation of arousal to being able to self-regulate is a process that begins in infancy and continues through early childhood. The caregiver's role in this process is extensive; initially, the provision of food, clothing, and physical soothing assists the infant in (emotional) state regulation; later, more complex communications and interactions with the caregiver teach the child to manage distress, control impulses, and delay gratification (p. 4).*

Thus, self-regulation can be seen as a gradual process that relies primarily on the success of the early secure and trusting relationship between the caregiver and the child. In the beginning, the infant relies on the caregiver to regulate situations for them when they are upset, frightened, or hungry. Then the child progressively develops the self-regulation skills himself as he interacts with peers and others, eventually achieving an emotional life independent of the first primary caregivers (Warhol, 1998). This process critically impacts a child's mental health development.

Key 4: Teach self-regulation skills.

Wisdom from the Field

Children who have difficulty with self-control face other difficulties as well, as they interact with others in the child-care community. Early childhood practitioners in a university teacher preparation program were asked about children who have a lack of control over their emotional expression. They reported seeing the following outcomes as a result of the impact of poor self-regulation skills on children's relationships with others:

- Other children will avoid contact or will choose not to play with a child who does not regulate his emotional outburst or reactions.

- Children who tend to cry at the drop of a hat, or get mad easily, have a hard time keeping friends.

- One little boy who would frequently call the other children names and hit them when he was frustrated began to be excluded by other children from any play situation.

- A little girl who cried easily and got upset frequently was avoided by other children who were leery of playing with her, fearful about upsetting her.

- Children quickly learn which children may become aggressive if they do not get their way. The child who uses aggression as an emotional response will be avoided as much as possible.

Strategies to help young children gain emotional regulation skills

For the early childhood practitioner, tools for enhancing emotional regulation for young children are crucial for supporting children's mental health. This question was posed to several groups of early childhood teachers and child-care providers in an early childhood classroom: How can we enhance emotional regulation for children in our programs? The following strategies come from their experience in the field and a solid knowledge of culturally and developmentally appropriate practice.

- Teach specific methods to control impulses, like "Stop and wait," "Slow down, stop, and think," and "Take a deep breath, count to five, say 'calm down.'"

- Model appropriate reactions to your own feelings and then explain to the children why you did what you did.

- Teach children how to control their emotions in different situations through role play or dramatic play.

- Help children learn to recognize each other's emotions through role play or with expression flash cards.

- Help children understand how they are feeling, and how other people are feeling by exploring facial expressions and body language. Also, give them facial expressions and body language to use when they are feeling frustrated, angry, or impatient.

- Always <u>respect</u> children's feelings; never minimize a feeling.

- Build close relationships and establish trust with each child.

- Acknowledge when they are successful at self-control.

- Practice specific skills for coping with fear and anxiety before they encounter stressful situations.

- Teach children that everything is not a disaster—help them learn to distinguish 'big' events from common daily interactions.

- Encourage problem solving skills by using questions like, "What can I do to help you calm yourself down?"

Other Strategies for Increasing Self-Regulation

There are many commercial tools on the market that help children learn to express emotions and practice self-regulation skills, as well as activities that can be modified to be part of many child care programs. One familiar activity is dramatic play. With preschoolers, you can write short plays that help teach "What I do if I am … angry, sad, happy" and have the children act them out. If a child is excited about an upcoming vacation, for instance, how do they contain some of that exuberance with the other children instead of running all around the room hugging friends? Children can offer their own strategies and adapt as they go. In addition, teach children relaxation skills to use when they are upset or frustrated like taking deep and slow breaths together as a class, or one-on-one with a child who is getting over-stimulated. Helping children 'check their own engines' is another strategy that aids in their recognition of how their body changes as stress level increases: *Is your engine running fast? Is your heart beating faster? How can we slow your engine down, slow, slow, slow. Breathe deeply.* Also, many children have problems with self-regulation because they do not have a good foundation for problem-solving. Board games or flash cards can teach problem-solving skills to children. Exercises like "Stop, Relax, and Think" or variations of this can be very effective, especially if practiced at times when no child is upset. There are many children's books on the market today that deal with how children can handle various stressful situations. Reading books during circle time reinforces concepts the caregiver is practicing with role play or dramatic play. Whatever strategies are employed, provide them in a non-threatening atmosphere so children will feel okay about sharing their feelings and reactions with others.

Problem-solving skills for children include:

- Negotiating (I'll give you this if you give me that.)

- Compromising (You can do it for 5 minutes and then I can do it for 5 minutes.)

- Recognizing and appreciating differences (You are faster than me but I can hop, so let's be partners in the sack race.)

- Generating alternatives (Instead of doing it this way, how else could we do it?)

- Resolving conflict through discussion, peer mediation, "talking sticks" (I get to offer a solution, and then you do. We will decide which solution works best for both of us, or a friend will make the final decision.)

- Language usage (For example, using "or" for solutions: this or that would work; "some" or "all" as in this might work for some, but not all of us.)

- If/then consequences (If I do this, then this will happen.)

- Perspective taking (You feel this way because you....)

Environmental Strategies

Kimmy entered the toddler play area shyly, still clinging to her mom. Four other toddlers were playing with Legos® or stuffed animals. After a couple of minutes, Kimmy ventured a few feet from her mom and picked up a toy phone, saying, "Hi mommy."

The environment of the child-care program can be a valuable asset in helping children with their self-regulation skills. Practitioners need to look objectively at their setting for sensory input that may be stressing those children with a low threshold for sounds, smells, or noise, for example. If a room has overhead fluorescent lights that buzz, it may impact how well a child with sensory processing difficulties can manage his reactions to interactions with others. Even children who typically manage their sensory processing well can become overwhelmed with too much stimulation. Having a keen outlook on our setting can prevent some behaviors from occurring that are a result of a child losing control. In the same way, our environments can enhance a child's ability to self-regulate if it is perceived by the child to be a safe and secure place with adults she can trust and rely on.

Another environmental strategy is to incorporate a soft spot in the child care setting (Brouette, 2004). Soft spots are areas where a child can go to relax, regroup, regain control of her feelings. It might include a small sofa, pillows, puppets or other quiet toys, and soft lighting. Let the children know what the soft spot is used for and set some basic guidelines, such as how many children may use it at a time, etc. You can also have 'mini' soft spots throughout your setting, like clusters of pillows in different areas that give children a resting spot or a place to regroup. This is a proactive intervention for helping children learn to regulate themselves, that is relatively easy to implement.

So much of what we see as maladaptive behaviors in adults may stem from missing out early in life in emotional regulation skill development. In children who strike out against others, as in the school shootings that have happened in recent years, the ability to regulate the impulse to hurt someone else is not checked. Emotional regulation skills help a child problem-solve other solutions, and help them stop and check the impulse to harm others. It cannot be overemphasized how important this skill is for young children to master. Impulse control is vital for expressing emotions in a healthy manner and for enhancing strong and positive mental health.

Summary

What a valuable gift to give to children, the ability to regulate their feelings of anger, fear, or stress. This is something early childhood educators can teach them: how to handle stress, how to get rid of anger, how to share happiness and joy. It is also a life-long gift. Later successful relationships with peers and within the community will depend on a child knowing his own feelings and how to regulate them with the skills he learned in early childhood.

Key Points:

1. An important emotional achievement for children in early childhood, and crucial to their positive mental health development, is developing the ability to regulate their own emotions and feelings.

2. Self-regulation is a gradual process that relies primarily on the success of the early secure and trusting relationship between the caregiver and the child.

3. Emotional regulation is important for helping children make and keep friends and develop a positive self-view.

4. The physical and emotional environment of the child-care program can be a valuable asset in helping children with their self-regulation skills.

5. A lack of self-regulating ability can have an adverse affect on a child's learning, social relationships, and self-esteem.

6. Strategies can be implemented throughout the early childhood setting that encourage emotional self-regulation skill development.

Chapter 5

What it Means to be At Risk
Key 5: Support and enhance resilience.

So How Are the Children?

People who work in various areas of human services, like crisis nursery program staff, or child protection workers, often see children in some of the worst possible situations: homeless, hungry, neglected, frightened. They find that some children seem to be able to weather the uncertainly of their difficult young lives with such finesse, it's almost uncanny; others struggle with their losses and their lack of stability by displaying mistrust and challenging behaviors. These same children may be part of a child-care setting. We refer to children who are in situations of substantiated child neglect or abuse—or in danger of it—as "at risk." The risk for the child may be in any

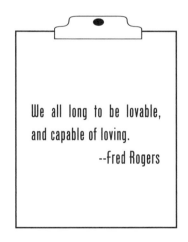

We all long to be lovable, and capable of loving.
--Fred Rogers

developmental domain: physical, cognitive, social, and emotional. The child may have behavior challenges, an assessed disability, or be living in an environment with risk factors that can affect their healthy growth and development. In the past many believed that very young children were "safe" from the effects of traumatic events because they were too young to realize what was happening; now, research shows that an infant's developing brain is indeed taking in information from the environment and responding to the feedback. According to research by Groves (2007), this knowledge of a baby's sensitivity to traumatic events happening in their environment increases the importance of our recognition of significant stressors in their lives, and our work to eliminate or diffuse them.

The role of resiliency then, becomes a critical factor in how children who are at risk will handle stress, react or adapt to negative situations, and overcome obstacles to their attainment of healthy mental health. Resilience, described in depth later in this chapter, is the individual's ability to adapt successfully when exposed to risk factors that may be biological or environmental. We will see further in this chapter how many children are being faced with biological and environmental risk factors and how our work with them in the early childhood setting can increase their resilience against these factors.

Risk in the United States

The statistics for children facing risk in their physical, social, and emotional development are staggering. In the United States, every 10 seconds a child is abused or neglected; some estimate over a million cases a year. The National Child Traumatic Stress Network (2005) found in children ages 12 to 17, that 8 percent had been victims of sexual abuse, 17 percent physical abuse, and 30 percent had experienced the emotional trauma of witnessing violence. The Children's Defense Fund (2005) reports that every 10 seconds in America a child is abused or neglected. Infants and toddlers fare the worst by age group when it comes to maltreatment. According to Cook (2007), 76% of children who died from abuse in 2004 were under the age of four. The risks to a child who is in a violent or neglectful setting are tremendous and can have lifelong implications on their mental health. Research shows that a child in an abusive or neglectful environment is at high risk for a variety of emotional issues, including attachment disorders and emotional disturbances. Children exposed to violence can lose their trust in their primary caregiver, who has shown they can't or won't protect them, giving way to a break in the attachment relationship, which is so important to a child's self-concept and overall emotional well-being. Cook (2007) found that children who experience repetitive harm or rejection by a primary caregiver develop a sense of themselves as being powerless, ineffective, and unlovable. This leads to an expectation in the child of rejection by others, further cycling the child toward diminished self-value and lower belief in his own competencies. A child who is living in an environment where there is no reasonable expectation of safety will find it difficult to recover the lost sense of security that is a building block to forming relationships. Unfortunately, Shaw and Goode (2005) found infants and toddlers to be the fastest growing age group removed from their homes due to abuse or neglect. Do we need a better reason to make sure the early childhood setting gives children all we have to ensure that their emotional development is not only enhanced, but in fact protected and secured? The experiences of early childhood can greatly enhance or damage the mental health of young children.

Increase in Mental Health Issues in Young People

National statistics make clear that mental health issues are on the increase for American youth. The U.S. Surgeon General recently reported that about 20 percent of children and teenagers will experience a mental health problem. (Consortium Connections, 2006). We already know that children who have a mental health issue will face a higher risk of behavioral, social, and academic problems. Children with untreated mental health disorders face an even bleaker future, particularly in their relationships with peers, family, and in their school experiences. According to the Consortium Connections, children with severe emotional needs have twice as high a dropout rate as children without mental health issues.

In addition to the mental health implications of children exposed to overwhelming stressors in their young lives, there are other concerns as well. According to research from Johnson & Knitzer (2006) at the National Center on Poverty, disrupted emotional development has a direct impact on early school failure. In fact, up to one third of all young children in the United States are at risk for early school failure, despite all the calls for school readiness and educational reform. The National Center on Poverty Study revealed poverty as the greatest risk factor for children. The study also names poor quality early care and learning experiences as the second major set of risk factors for children in the U.S. (Johnson and Knitzer, 2006). Chapter 1 discussed at length the research that supports quality early education programming and its importance to children's emotional development. We know from extensive studies what helps children and what harms them in early development.

Six-year-old Ramone and 8-year-old Deshawn are going to a crisis nursery shelter home for respite care. The caseworker asks, "Are you nervous about anything? Do you want to ask me any questions about where you are going?" Ramone says, "Will they know we can't eat shrimp?" "Yes," says the caseworker, "they will know that, and you will be safe there."

Children Described as At Risk

As we have discussed earlier, children are at risk when they have biological (internal) or environmental (external) stressors that impact their development in any of the major domains: physical, cognitive, social, or emotional. We are concerned here with the emotional area of growth and development influenced in a number of ways. According to the Surgeon General of the United States (2005), 13 percent of U.S. children have anxiety disorders, 6.2 percent have mood disorders, and 10.3 percent have disruptive disorders. Also, at any given time in the U.S., between 10 and 15 percent of children show symptoms of depression, and of those, 20-40 percent will develop bipolar disorder. We know from research that low-birth-weight infants (internal stressor) are at an increased risk for behavioral and emotional problems. In addition, research shows that infants of mothers who are depressed for one year following birth (external stressor) will be at risk for behavioral, physiological, and biochemical dysregulation as they grow (Warhol, 1998). Children who are at risk because of internal and external stressors are five times more likely to later become juvenile offenders, according to some studies (Lifetime Effects: The High/Scope Perry Preschool Project, 2005). Dr. Martha Farrell Erickson, developmental psychologist at the Center of Early Education and Development at the University of Minnesota, puts it this way: "There are several negative implications if a baby is not attended to or given the kind of attention necessary. The child will not properly develop the capacity to self-comfort or manage other emotions necessary for healthy development" (Kaufmann, 2005). Children who are at risk face challenges to their emotional development that, without intervention, can negatively impact their mental health in childhood or young adulthood. The previous chapter offered greater detail into risks for children who do not develop self-regulatory skills.

In addition to these sobering statistics, experts believe that 5 million children each year in the United States experience some form of traumatic experience. The Diagnostic and Statistical Manual of Mental Disorders (DSM) defines a traumatic event as one where both of the following are present: 1) the person experiences, witnesses, or is confronted with an event/events that involves actual or threatened death or serious injury, or a threat to the physical integrity of self or others; and 2) the person's response involves intense fear, helplessness, or horror. A traumatic experience for a child is an event that substantially alters her view of the world or her place in the world. Such an experience includes, but is not limited to, abuse and neglect, family breakup, illness, and even natural disasters such as a hurricane. In the aftermath of Hurricane Katrina in 2005, thousands of children lost their homes, family members, everything familiar to them, without any warning or preparation. We see how traumatic events in the life of a child can create a stress that threatens a child's core emotional development. In the Winter 2007 issue of *Focal Point,* the article "Traumatic Stress and Child Welfare" emphasized that untreated traumatic stress in young children can multiply problems for them in every area of functioning, including their cognition, attention, and mental health. Thus, the child will use their emotional and physical energy for coping and survival instead of what is typical for children of the same age: learning to explore their world with safety and security.

The role of this text is not to teach mental health interventions, but rather to teach methods of improving our environments and programming in early childhood to enhance mental health and emotional development for young children, particularly those who may be experiencing risk factors that could harm their mental health. Referral to appropriate resources is paramount for a child's well-being when a child care practitioner suspects a mental health disorder, or red flags point to issues in emotional development. Local mental health organizations, city and county government mental health agencies, public health agencies, as well as special education early intervention services are referral sources for families. Early intervention for mental health needs is critical for a child's short and long-term outcomes.

Children who are experiencing crisis are at risk in their healthy emotional development, which we have already seen can impact them for the rest of their lives. The remainder of this chapter will focus on risk factors and strategies for increasing resiliency in children who face risk factors.

Internal and External Risk Factors

Research has helped shed light on many of the internal and external stressors that put young children at risk. *Stressors* are the demands placed on an individual that can be greater than his resources to cope with the event, whether it is biological in nature (as in a disability) or external (as in neglect). Stress is an important factor in children's mental health. If it becomes overwhelming, it can cause a child to "shut down," disabling his coping abilities. An accumulation of stressful factors can lead to serious mental health impairments in children, including depression and anxiety disorders. Also, a child whose risk factors become part of a traumatic event in his life may develop Post Traumatic Stress Disorder ("Mental Health," 2006). These conditions will require professional interventions, the earlier the better.

In *Starting Smart: How Early Experiences Affect Brain Development,* Hawley (2000), the brief identifies the role of stress early on in an infant's experiences:

> *One of the most fundamental tasks an infant undertakes is determining whether and how he can get his needs met in the world in which he lives. He is constantly assessing whether his cries for food and comfort are ignored or lovingly answered, whether he is powerless or can influence what adults do. If the adults in his life respond predictably to his cries and provide for his needs, the infant will be more likely to use these adults as sources of safely and security. With his safety taken care of, he then can focus his attention on exploring, allowing his brain to take in all the wonders of the world around him. If, however, his needs are met only sporadically and pleas for comfort are usually ignored or met with harsh words and rough handling, the infant will focus his energies on ensuring that his needs are met. He will have more and more difficulty interacting with people and objects in his environment, and his brain will shut out the stimulation it needs to develop healthy cognitive and social skills.*

An infant, in the setting described above, begins life at a deficit when it comes to his emotional security. Without the responsive caregiving described in earlier chapters helping her to cope with stress, she will have difficulty with attachment and trust. As the child becomes a preschooler, exploration may be inhibited as will the learning that accompanies experimentation and exploration in new situations. The preschooler may be reluctant to play with others, share, participate in dramatic play with peers, and so begins to lose ground in emotional growth and maturity appropriate for her age. Empathy, a learned skill that comes from interactions with others under the model of a trusted and consistent caregiver, will be hard to achieve. Self-regulation, necessary for success in social relationships, will be difficult to master without requisite earlier emotional building blocks like security, trust, and positive and responsive support by a caregiver. Stress becomes a stumbling block for positive mental health for infants, toddlers, and preschoolers.

Stress shows up in other facets of a child's life that may not signify a traumatic event. As previously indicated, there is a difference in the types of stressors a child may experience. Internal stressors are biological factors, such as low birth rate. External stressors are environmental and include being born into poverty. Groves (2007) places child stressors on a continuum "ranging from short-term, tolerable or even beneficial stress to prolonged, uncontrollable stress that is traumatic or toxic to child development" (p. 2). He also explains that prolonged exposure to stressors can result in damage to a child's ability to respond to stress and may even result in smaller brain development. The Grantmakers in Health (2005) in a policy brief on the impact of trauma in young children, also found a key relationship between brain development and stressors. For instance, a child exposed to high levels of stress and anxiety had some areas of their brains overdeveloped, while other brain functions necessary for learning were underdeveloped. They also found children exposed to trauma had higher rates of allergies, asthma, and gastrointestinal issues, in addition to future mental health issues tied to early trauma. A child may experience stressors from any of the following internal and external factors:

Internal factors:

- Low birth weight
- Disability
- Prenatal substance abuse
- Abuse of pregnant mother
- Prenatal malnutrition
- No prenatal vitamins
- High delivery complications

External factors:

- Unresponsive caregiving by primary caregiver
- Parental mental illness
- Poverty
- Being born to a mother who did not graduate from high school
- Being born without health insurance
- Family violence
- Chronic neglect
- Being born to a teen mother
- Being born to a mother who received late or no prenatal care
- Poor nutrition

Other Mental Health Implications

In the landmark book *Ghosts from the Nursery,* Karr-Morse and Wiley (1997) make frightening correlations between a child's early years and later violent behavior as an adult. One of their key findings in studying adult offenders and adults who did not become violent in spite of being at risk, is the fact that as children non-violent adults developed their ability to trust and to feel connected to the people around them. This is one of the core milestones of healthy emotional development, as we saw in Chapter 1. On the other hand, Karr-Morse and Wiley state: "While we might like to believe that given sufficient opportunity we can reverse any damage done to children, the research tells us that the effects of some early experiences cannot be undone" (p. 21). They point to "critical periods" where a child can be impacted for the positive, and that period may be brief and, once closed, forever lost to the child. Again, this highlights the critically important role the early childhood practitioner plays in building positive mental health in children at risk. If a child who is at risk can be nurtured early in a responsive environment, there is a greater chance that the child will develop mastery of emotional milestones critical to later success in life. No one can overestimate the role that quality caregiving has on children.

In fact, when Mason-Dixon Polling and Research asked law enforcement professionals from across the country how to reduce youth violence and crime, they overwhelmingly (70 percent) said that the best strategy is quality early childhood and school-age programs for children (Saffrin and Kilian, 2005).

Early childhood practitioners are in a unique position to improve the odds for children who have experienced trauma or are at risk because of other stressors. Responsive caregiving strategies encourage trust-building and enhance resilience. In addition, early childhood educators and practitioners can play a key role in referral to parents of early detection and intervention services in their communities. A child who is at risk may qualify for some services through early intervention and the family may qualify for family-based services.

Key 5: Support and enhance resilience.

Resilience is the ability to cope successfully in difficult circumstances, such as abusive situations, neglect, war, and poverty. In addition, some children may function well in some areas of their development and show deficits in others (Cook, 2007). Kaiser (2003) points out that research has found four basic characteristics in children who are resilient in the face of at-risk settings. These four characteristics are:

1. Social competence
2. Problem-solving skills
3. Autonomy and self-esteem
4. Sense of purpose and future

Social competence refers to a child's ability to engage in a positive way with people around them. So, as a skill set, it means a child can communicate well, has a sense of humor, is flexible, and can translate that behavior into getting along with others and being accepted. Social competence can be seen as a result of a child's core temperament (flexible vs. feisty or hard-to-warm-up) but also as a skill learned in a social context. The natural ability of a child is enhanced in social settings where their skills are encouraged and reinforced by peers and caregivers. *Problem-solving skills* in children who are resilient means the ability to plan, adjust to changes, anticipate consequences, and as Kaiser (2003) notes, ask for help. Again, problem-solving skills can be seen as due to both innate characteristics (high on a temperament scale on approach and adaptability) and also as a learned attribute gained in the social setting. *Autonomy and self-esteem* as a skill for resiliency means that the child believes in his own capabilities and will use those capabilities to do what he needs to do in order to get by or get through a difficulty. We saw in Chapter

3 that children are born with a natural predisposition to have either a positive or negative mood. Resilient children believe in themselves, which seems to come from within and is encouraged and grown through supportive relationships with caregivers. Finally, a *sense of purpose and future* represents a key finding: a child who is optimistic about the future tends to be more resilient. This child will believe, even in the face of great odds, that she can be successful. Such sense of purpose is tied to core temperament traits of positive mood, approach, and adaptability.

A Sense of Purpose and Future

The first three characteristics of resiliency are easily influenced in the external; they can be enhanced by what we do in our child-care settings. The last one, a sense of optimism for the future, is partly how a child is wired from birth with the temperament trait of positive mood. Some children, in spite of circumstances, never seem to fuss or be dissatisfied, even as infants. We have all known children who were only whiny when they were sick and that's why we suspected they were in fact ill. Other children seem to never be happy, in spite of full tummies, lots of comforting, and responsive care. As noted in Chapter 3, mood is one of the nine temperament traits and is measured on a temperament scale from 1 to 10 as negative, positive, or somewhere in between. This is a natural personality trait that all children are born with. Temperament is considered by child developmentalists to be about half biological and half environmental. So a child may come "wired" a certain way from birth, but can still learn to make adjustments given the right tools by providers and other caregivers.

Optimism, although an inborn personality trait, can be encouraged in a child by an early childhood provider through a variety of methods. A child who is responded to, particularly early on, with consistent delight, is going to begin to feel good about their effect on others. Children who are given a chance to be successful will also feel more optimistic. There are many opportunities in the child-care day to help a child feel successful. Glasser and Easley (1998), in *Transforming the Difficult Child,* details several strategies for creating success for a child who may not have experienced it before. Each created success can then be reinforced with encouragement by the caregiver, thus increasing the effectiveness of the successful moment. Creating success for a child is only limited by a caregiver's imagination. Also, a setting that is safe and secure, with consistent routines, can help a child release some fears and anxieties related to inconsistent settings or care. As the child begins to believe that the setting will remain constant, that toys are in the same place today that they were yesterday, that Miss Emily is here today and she was here yesterday, then he can begin to trust in the future. The child will expect that tomorrow will be like today in her child care home. This initiates a slow process of building of hope and trust in the future.

Jerell sat happily in her car seat as her nanny drove around town, running errands. She stopped at the bank and post office, each time taking Jerell out of the car seat and carrying her into the business, then back out to the car to be buckled into the car seat. They continued this action for more than an hour without a whine from Jerell, who seemed content to just be riding along.

The important role of the early childhood educator and caregiver cannot be overemphasized when we are looking at helping build resilience in children at risk. While some factors are out of the control of the child-care provider—natural temperament, past traumatic events, the environment outside of childcare—there are many factors within the control of the early childhood setting. Cook (2007) points out that the child/caregiver relationship is an important indicator of a child's resilience when the relationship is a positive attachment and when the caregiver is supportive and competent. The early childhood practitioner can effect a child's development of a positive sense of themselves and their value to the world around them. The *Crisis Manual for the Early Childhood Classroom* gives practitioners the following strategies and guidelines for encouraging resilience in the children we work with:

Four strategies to encourage resilience in all children:

1. Take time to know each of the children in your program.
2. Observe them. Use behavioral assessment forms that are developed just for early childhood educators.
3. Have children talk about their feelings.
4. Make sure that children feel safe in your setting. Talk to them about being safe there.

These strategies can help you frame your own needs assessment for a child who may be at risk in their emotional development because of external and internal stressors. You can determine how you need to adapt programming to meet an individual need, how to raise concerns with the family, and when to make a referral to another agency if circumstances warrant intervention. National mental health resources are available at the end of this book. You can contact your local mental health organizations, county mental health and public health agencies, and school district for referral and program information to share with parents in your program. Early intervention is crucial for a child who is at risk and can be implemented both in your early childhood program adaptations and by the mental health professionals whom parents may contact.

Wisdom from the Field

Resilience is something that a child may partially be born with, but, as seen above, can also be encouraged and enhanced by the early childhood practitioner through their relationship with the child. Early childhood practitioners asked to elaborate on the four strategies to encourage resilience in children, listed earlier in the chapter, had some practical applications: (*#1: Take time to know each of the children in your program*). The child must trust the caregiver in order for the relationship to be effective. A strong, responsive, consistent relationship between the child care practitioner and the child will enable the provider to enact the strategies to encourage and support resilience. (*#2: Observe them. Use behavioral assessment forms that are developed just for early childhood educators.*) Early childhood practitioners need to practice observation and recording of every child in their program, consistently. Red flags become more evident when there is a written record of the child's development. Early childhood teachers often report that they see the beginning signs of developmental issues early on when they are using recording forms. Some training is available on specific social and emotional checklists and assessments, though they may not be widely available or affordable. Contact a local child care resource and referral agency or mental health agencies for information in your area. (*#3: Have children talk about their feelings.*) Child care providers can implement many strategies for helping children learn and talk about their feelings, including dramatic play, role play, commercially produced board games and card games, and story books. One early educator in a

Head Start classroom had people's faces with various expressions glued onto long tongue depressors and kept them in a bucket in the classroom. Children felt free to express their feelings with the expression sticks if they liked. (*#4: Make sure that children feel safe in your setting. Talk to them about being safe there.*) For at-risk children, the child care setting may be their most consistent and secure environment. Talk to all kids about their safety and security while they are in their classroom or child care home. Repeat often, "You are safe here. I will keep you safe." Make sure that within your environment there are small, quiet places where a child may go to regroup or nestle in, while always in sight. Keep toys and equipment consistent, putting them away in the same place each night so it is where children remember it the next morning. Having their own place, like a cubbie, to store personal items can also encourage a sense of safety and belonging.

Building a Sense of Belonging to a Community

A final strategy for strengthening resilience for young children is to build a sense of community and belonging within the child care program. When a child feels he belongs to the community, he then has a stake in the outcomes of the community. Early childhood providers are in a unique position to support children through the child care program by encouraging family involvement, by having each child bring some personal items to the setting, and by bringing in outside members of the larger community to talk about their various roles (teachers, firefighters, doctors, etc.). Children who have jobs and responsibilities within the program become invested in their special community of child care. If they have a role in choosing the program's rules, they are part of the process of making sure their community functions well. Self-esteem grows as the child sees the importance of his role in the overall health and well being of his community. This in turn builds a sense of altruism and a care for the "greater good" outside of the individual. As a child grows in an emotionally healthy manner, he will learn to care about the community, even when it means sacrifice on his part. This is important as we prepare children to be citizens of the world. Sometimes the greater good may involve a lack of self-interest and self-motivation for the sake of something greater. More information will be provided in the final chapter of this book on the practitioner's toolbox for working with children to enhance emotional development by building a sense of community.

Summary

Children face many risks today from both internal and external stressors. The early childhood community can provide many protective factors for children that boost their resilience and help them cope with events in their lives that will have an impact on their emotional growth and development.

Key Points:

1. Children are at risk when they have external or internal stressors that can impact their development in any of the major domains: physical, cognitive, social, and emotional.

2. Stressors can be seen as demands placed on an individual that can overwhelm his resources to cope with the demands, whether biological or external.

3. Resilience can be defined as the ability to cope successfully in difficult circumstances, such as abusive or neglectful situations, war, or poverty.

4. Some factors are out of the control of the child care provider, such as natural temperament, past traumatic events, or the environment outside of childcare. But there are many factors within the control of early childhood settings for building resilience in a child at risk.

5. Building a community within the child care program is critically important to increasing resilience in young children

6. If a child who is at risk can be nurtured early in a responsive environment, there is a greater chance that the child will develop mastery of emotional milestones critical to later success in life.

Chapter 6

Making and Keeping Friends

Key 6: Teach friendship skills.

The Relationship Between Emotional and Social Development

As we've seen in previous chapters, how successfully children master the stages and milestones of emotional development will have a great impact on their relationships with others, especially their peers. These important relationships will in turn impact their mental health outcomes as they grow. Healthy and appropriate skills are a key to social successes: if you don't know how to navigate through all the social signals, you will have a hard time making or keeping friends. A child that is very boisterous and physical may not realize that his quiet friend doesn't like so much noise in the reading area, and the friend may begin to avoid her peer.

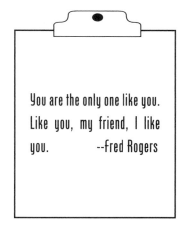

You are the only one like you. Like you, my friend, I like you.   --Fred Rogers

Besides the ability to read social cues, how well a child learns self-regulation skills will have a major impact on their friendships. For instance, a child who cannot control aggressiveness and hits a neighbor when he feels frustrated will find that his is often playing alone. The child who has learned to maneuver through the social situations with greater finesse, knowing when to enter a play group or when to take the lead, will find that other children like to play with him. Additionally, this type of social cueing can have longer range impact: research shows that children who are judged more positively by their peers are more likely to perform better academically (Sparling, Meunier and Crooms, 2006), thus tying social and emotional influences to academic outcomes. There has been a great deal written about children's social skill development, among them the classic *Fostering Children's Social Competence* (Katz and McClellan, 1997) which is recommended for further study. This chapter will look at the interplay of emotional skill development and social skills as they influence a child's overall mental health outcomes.

Aggression and Social Relationships

Long ago, Aristotle said, "Who would choose to live, even if possessed with all other things, without friends?" The philosopher understood that health and well-being is dependent on many factors, including friendships. In my interviews with early childhood teachers and caregivers, one of the most frequently cited reasons they give for children not wanting to play with other children is the lack of self-control on one child's part. Early on, the toddler who bites or hits will find himself avoided by most of the other toddlers who have been on the receiving end of the aggression. If there is no intervention, the child may continue the aggressive behaviors while his isolation increases. Isolation will only accentuate the frustration he may be feeling, further increasing aggression. In this cycle of aggressive, non-social behavior and its negative consequences, the child will lose out on the benefits of the social interactions that would teach more appropriate play skills such as conflict resolution and problem-solving. As he continues friendless, his social isolation will inhibit other emotional growth such as cooperation and empathy. This sets the stage for the risk of emotional disturbances including defiance, non-compliance, and other behavioral challenges as the child's self-image plummets.

The significance of emotional skill deficits and the impact on social development is borne out in recent research done by the National Institute of Child Health and Development (NICHD). In the Study of Early Child Care and Youth Development, a longitudinal study, Campbell et al (2006), examined social outcomes related to the aggressive behaviors of children from age 9 through 12. They classified children by their level of physical aggression as identified by a parent. The outcome data was drawn from teacher observation records and from children's self reporting. The authors offered the following significant results regarding aggression and its relationship to social skill development:

> *Children on the high-stable aggression trajectory [my emphasis] (3% of sample) showed the most severe adjustment problems, including poorer social skills, higher levels of externalizing problems, and more self-reported peer problems; those on the moderate-stable aggression trajectory (15%) showed poor regulation and inattention. Although children with moderate levels of early aggression that decreased sharply by school entry (12%) appeared well adjusted at follow-up, those who showed a low level of stable aggression (25%) evidenced some unanticipated social and behavior problems. Children in the contrast group (45%) were consistently very low in aggression from toddlerhood onward (Campbell et al, 2006).*

These study results show important links between levels of aggression in children and its relationship to their social skills acquisition in important areas such as getting along with peers and self control. Aggressiveness often leads to subsequent lack of success in peer relationships. The researchers further found that even low aggression, when it is consistent, is a risk factor for social problems in children. For example, we understand that a child who takes toys away from other children, though not overtly aggressive, will begin to be viewed by peers as a less desirable friend. The research supports what early childhood practitioners see every day in child care programs: correlation between emotional competencies like self-regulation and problem-solving and social success for children. A child who does not know how to use her words instead of kicking or hitting will end up isolated from peers.

A Teacher's Story

I have seen first-hand how important emotional regulation is for social competence. One of my 3-year-olds entered the school year as a "rejected" child from three other programs, even though it was his first year in preschool. Kenny was an anxious child who cried and whined at a drop of a hat. If another child did not share, or if Kenny accidentally dropped something he would go into instant melt down. He would pull his hands to his chest, rolling them together while with lowered eyes he repeated over and over again, "I sorry." That behavior got him labeled by his parents, grandparents, and other teachers as a "behavior problem." On the first day in my program, his mom told me I could punish him or spank him if he needed it. I used that opportunity to tell them that my classroom was a "safe zone" and that together we would help Kenny learn skills and language to help him self-regulate. She did not believe me but heard me out. It took a lot of one-on-one work with Kenny and it meant my having to do intentional modeling and skill building for him, other children, his family and yes…my aide. The aide did not believe Kenny "wanted" to stop his behaviors and that he provoked others to treat him badly because he "got the attention he was seeking."

I was able to reach Kenny and help him to learn skills, words and techniques to self-regulate. It took a few months and lots of time observing, assessing, and following an individualized behavior plan, as well as meeting with my staff, his family, and the other students. By age 4, Kenny became a secure, loving and friendly student. He gained his confidence and entered kindergarten ready for school, socially accepted by his peers and family. Kenny is the student who taught me the true meaning of being a teacher. Kenny is a great example of why emotional regulation is so essential for social competency. (permission to print, Buch W.).

The Need for Social Relationships

Kenny is not so different from many of the children we work with in early childhood settings. Often, challenging behaviors are the result of children who do not know how to handle their own feelings and frustrations as they interact with other children. They desire friendships, relationship, and belonging to the community, but they are often excluded from the social relationships they seek because of their behaviors related to a lack of emotional regulatory skills. The social relationship can be out of reach because they have poor social skill development. The Social-Emotional Development in Young Children (2003), a Guide developed by the Michigan Department of Community Health, has done extensive work in assessing the social and emotional development needs of young children. They found that intimate and caring relationships form the framework for all meaningful social development. An excerpt from the research study shows that:

[A child's healthy social development] begins in infancy, when infants respond to the familiar voice, smell and touch of the important people in their lives. When these first social experiences are rewarding, they support the next stage in social development. A toddler's excited exploration of new places is enabled by a secure relationship with a trusted adult who provides a base for the child's discoveries. Toddlers learn to share, cooperate, take turns, compromise and negotiate through relationships. A preschooler who looks up expectantly toward a parent when encountering an unexpected event depends on the adult's emotions for guidance about how to respond.... With adult support, preschool-age children learn more complex relationship skills including how to express personal views and opinions, how to discuss and resolve conflicts, and how to enjoy relationships (Michigan Department of Health, 2003).

The key to the child learning more complex friendship skills is the responsive relationship of a primary caregiver who models competencies and offers supportive care. From infancy to preschool, the child who has had a caring, nurturing, and supportive relationship is the child who has the building blocks for social aptitude.

Children also learn from their caregivers how to initiate and sustain successful relationships. If their models have been warm and responsive, as Kenny's teacher in the earlier section, they will have confidence to explore relationships with others in their social world. However, if they have had rejecting or unresponsive caregiving, they will be at risk when it comes to building social relationships because they will lack the necessary social competencies to initiate, engage, and respond to others in play settings.

Meredith held the Silly Putty® close to her side as Joachim asked her again if he could see it. She said, "I don't have to share with you." Miss Emily said, "Meredith, can we cut the Silly Putty® into two pieces?" Meredith replied, "Okay!"

Key 6: Teach friendship skills.

Social Competencies as Friendship Skills

Social competencies are those friendship skills which children need proficiency in so they can get along well in their social world. As they grow older, these social skills should also continue to develop, like knowing how to share, cooperate with others, and problem-solve a conflict among peers. Toddlers will behave differently than a preschooler but toddlers will have typical behaviors that other toddlers have. Social competence, the array of behaviors that permits one to develop and engage in positive interactions with peers, siblings, parents, and other adults (Sparling, Meunier and Crooms, 2006), will advance as children grow. Related to social competence is emotional competence, explained in Chapters 1 and 2, which is the ability to regulate emotions effectively to accomplish one's goals in ways that are acceptable to others. Social competencies depend on successful emotional competencies and are both closely intertwined.

Social competencies are also important as they relate to resilience and the support of positive mental health, particularly as a child grows up. Children begin with small steps of social skill aptitude and scaffold those to more complex skills. Friendship skills that are important to young children within their community include learning to listen to others, learning how to talk to others, understanding the feelings and actions of others, cooperation, and practicing conflict resolution. These are skills all children must learn if they are to succeed socially. The early childhood educator can teach them through modeling, peer interaction support, stories and role play, as well as direct social interventions. Peer interaction support, for example, is a strategy implemented by a teacher or caregiver as she watches children who may be struggling in play together; if two 24-month olds cannot navigate the cooperative skills needed to play side-by-side, the teacher might step in and initiate the cooperative move that keeps the play going smoothly. She may need to intervene more directly in a social interaction if two 4-year olds have tried to resolve a conflict that seems to be escalating rather than diffusing. She may approach with some options for resolution and give the children the opportunity to choose a mutually acceptable solution. As we have discussed earlier, friendship skills have a direct correlation to a child's mental health, particularly as the child grows up. Deficits in social skill development will also show up as deficits in emotional skill acquisition.

Stephens, in her article *Social Skills Children Need to Make and Keep Friends* (2002), observes that children need certain simple-to-complex skills in order to be successful in their social world. For example, it is fundamental that a child be able to "join" into play with others in a way that is agreeable to everyone; in order to accomplish this, a child must be aware of and share some common interests of others as well as be aware of the social cues that may be coming from the play partners. We have all seen the child who bursts into a play group and knocks over the blocks to the dismay of the other kids, or a child who sits on the fringe of a play group, not sure how to initiate the first move. Initiation into play with others is finessed when a child observes the activity and knows how to enter the social play with others. Part of this comes from social skills that include being able to listen to others, respect the feelings of peers, cooperate, and be inclusive. Stephens further posits that in order for a child to make and keep friends, she will need to practice the more sophisticated skills of empathizing with another child's perspective and practicing compassion. Additionally, the child must appear trustworthy in her willingness to help out her friends, no small feat for a child if her primary caregiver did not meet her own needs responsively. The community of a child-care program is a place where all children need to be taught belonging and affiliation skills; it is fundamental to their social success.

Wisdom from the Field

A cohort of early childhood professionals in a university teaching program were asked the question: *In your early childhood experience, how have you seen a child's emotional development impact their social behavior?* Their answers included:

- It affects how they make and keep friends.

- It affects how they get along with others in play situations.

- It also effects whether the child wants to repeat a similar experience with peers.

Then, in a follow-up question, they were asked, *What are your strategies for enhancing social skills through emotional mastery for young children?* The following are concrete and workable strategies from classrooms and family child care programs across the country:

- Play "feeling" games about different play situations, like "How would you feel if...." and "What would you do next?".

- Show children how to enter play by modeling the action steps and by giving them phrases to use. Consider using classroom rules like "You can't say, you can't play" (Katz and McClellan, 1997).

- Teach children to treat each other as they would want to be treated...reinforce this often.

- Give children the words to use to express feelings during play, like frustration or impatience with another child. Role-play situations that might come up and possible solutions.

- Make it safe for children to talk about their feelings by responding with nonjudgmental and affirming language.

- Give children tangible tools to get along with one another. Practice social skills like sharing and conflict resolution, with aids such as a "talking stick" or "conflict chair." For example, have two chairs that face each other in one part of the room where children are allowed to go to settle disputes. Rules need to be clear for "conflict chair" usage, such as, one person speaks at a time, each person gets to tell his part of the story, and a solution must be agreed on before they leave. Sometimes, a teacher may need to be involved with younger children in this process, but older children may be able to solve conflict through this method of looking for a workable solution. As much as possible, let children begin to resolve conflict without stepping in unless you are needed. A "talking stick" can be used in many ways as a device that allows each child a voice as they hold the stick.

- Realize that the teachers' own emotions and moods will have a definite impact on the classroom and the children. Be aware of how your own feelings may be influencing which children are asked to play and which may be left out.

In addition to the strategies above, early childhood practitioners can use the following techniques to support social competency in children specifically through *listening and talking* to others.

- Use mealtime and family-style dining to model intentional social skills, like sharing, passing, asking for more, etc.

- Take advantage of intentional small group activities such as circle time or discussion time to practice listening and conversation.

- Use reading groups that help provide communication skills between peers.

- Have individual conversations with children during activities, at the beginning of their day, or when they tell how school went that day. Review at the end of the day with each child.

- Read specific books to children about friendship.

- Present specific skill sets on how to talk to new friends, such as introducing oneself, asking the other person's name, asking if they want someone to play with, etc. You can individualize this to a particular child who may be struggling making friends.

- Give children openers and catch phrases to start conversations with others.

These strategies can help the early childhood educator intentionally promote constructive social interactions as well as support the emotional development of each child in their program by making sure that play is a successful event. In this way, play can be seen as instrumental in encouraging a child's positive mental health.

Travis was building a house at the Lego® table, by himself. Matthew rushed over and said, "I'm building a train" as he reached for a Lego® on Travis's house. Travis screamed, "That's mine!" and grabbed Matthew's hand. Matthew threw the Lego® to the other side of the room.

Role of the Child Care Practitioner

A child's social competencies are a key indicator of how well she will make friends in her world. As early childhood practitioners, we can work with children to encourage the acquisition of social competencies in a number of ways. We can begin by designing our learning and care environment to promote positive peer interactions and cooperative interactions. Placing the dramatic play area and equipment near the manipulatives or block area can encourage children to interact in new ways, like building a "house" where "families" are eating together. Placing quiet spaces next to a reading center can encourage children to sit by each other and read, or talk about stories together. Having enough equipment for all kids to adequately share is important to avoid conflicts over a popular toy or activity, in addition to ensuring that children can play a similar game or activity together. Children at different times will need space to make noise or be physical and also need quiet spaces. Separating these areas with physical structures like bookshelves or short dividers can help children join play when they want to and rest when needed. We can use social skills curricula that encourage relationship building as well as a sense of community which supports each child. Specific strategies for building a sense of community within the early childhood setting are included in the next chapter. We can also provide exercises and activities that assist children in scaffolding their play into more sophisticated roles which help them address relationship-building issues, such as dramatic play, board games, or story time. Even the simple skill of helping children learn how to enter a play group is important if a child is struggling socially. The early childhood practitioner has daily opportunities to impact a child's social development that can have life-long implications for success in school, success in future relationships, and success in how a child ultimately comes to view his role in the greater community around him.

Summary

Social relationships with peers are essential for the positive mental health of a child, including the ongoing development of a child's self-esteem and self-concept, problem-solving and conflict resolution skills, and the ability to engage in symbolic play that further reinforces a sense of self and belonging. Early childhood programs can promote social and emotional development through teaching and modeling friendship skills and social competencies in everyday activities and materials.

Key Points:

1. Children learn from their caregivers how to grow successful relationships with peers.

2. Social competencies are the skills children need to master in order to get along well in their social world.

3. The social competencies which young children need include learning to listen to others, learning how to talk to others, understanding the feelings and actions of others, cooperation, and practicing conflict resolution.

4. A child's self-regulation skills will have a major impact on the quality of their friendships.

5. A child with aggressive behaviors will experience isolation from peers if there is no intervention, which will accentuate the frustration, further increasing aggression.

6. If a child's caregivers have been warm and responsive, the child will have confidence to explore relationships with others.

7. Social relationships with peers are essential for a positive mental health, including the ongoing development of a child's self-esteem and self-concept, her problem-solving and conflict resolution skills, and her ability to engage in imaginary and dramatic play that reinforces her sense of self and belonging.

8. The early childhood practitioner has daily opportunities to impact a child's social development that can have life-long implications, for success in school, success in future relationships, and success in how a child ultimately comes to view his role in the greater community around him.

For Futher Reading

These books are useful resources for educators in helping children develop prosocial behaviors:

Evans, B. (2002). *You can't come to my birthday party! Conflict resolution with young children. Ypsilati, MI: High/Scope Press.*

Kemple, K. M. (2004). *Let's be friends: Peer competence and social inclusion in early childhood programs.* New York: Teachers College Press.

Levin, D. E. (2003). *Teaching young children in violent times: Building peaceable classroom.* Cambridge, MA: Educators for Social Responsibility and the National Association for the Education of Young Children.

Rice, J.A. (1995). *The kindness curriculum: Introducing young children to loving values. S*t. Paul: Redleaf Press.

Schomburg, R., Sharapan, H., & White, A. (2004). *Challenging behaviors: Where do we begin?* Pittsburgh, PA: Mister Rogers' Neighborhood and Family Communications.

Schomburg, R. Sharapan, H., White, A. (2001). *What do you do with the mad you feel? Helping children manage anger and learn self-control.* Pittsburgh, PA: Mister Rogers' Neighborhood and Family Communications.

Stern-LaRosa, C., & Bettman, E.H. (2004). *Hate hurts: How children learn and unleash prejudice.* New York: Scholastic.

Thomas, P. (2000). *Stop picking on me: A first look at bullying.* New York, NY: Scholastic.

WestEdCenter for Child and Family Studies. (2004). *The program for infant toddler caregivers trainer's manual. Module 1: Social-emotional growth and socialization.* Sacramento, CA: WestEd and California Department of Education.

Chapter 7

Tools for Promoting Children's Mental Health

Practical applications for skill development.

How do we encourage healthy development in our early childhood programs?

As we conclude the book, this chapter will discuss key applications to the skill development necessary for early childhood educators and caregivers to promote the positive emotional health of young children. As seen in earlier chapters, the mental health of a young child is clearly a predictor of future outcomes, from school readiness to healthy relationships with peers. The early years are the best time to intervene on behalf of children; we can impact their future with quality, responsive caregiving and early screening and assessment for emotional disorders. As seen in previous chapters, a child who is at risk for emotional disorders because of internal or external stressors (such as neglect, abuse, disability, etc.) will benefit from a high quality early childhood experience though more intense mental health intervention may be necessary for the best outcomes. Awareness of early intervention services in your community is important information to share with families if you have concerns about a

> What do you do with the mad that you feel when you feel so mad you could bite? ... Do you punch a bag?/Do you pound some clay or some dough?/Do you round up friends for a game of tag?/Or see how far you can go?/It's great to be able to stop when you've planned a thing that's wrong .... --Fred Rogers

child's development or if you have found risk indicators using an emotional/behavioral early childhood checklist tool. Many such tools are available commercially for child-care programs. The validity of the tool and the preparation of the person using the checklist are important considerations for a child-care program in examining whether they will employ checklists as part of their regular observation and recording of young children's development. If a decision is made to incorporate mental health screening in programming, then steps need to be in place for how and to whom the information will be shared. Keep in mind that not all parents will be receptive to learning that you have concerns about their child's development. Parents may be reluctant to have a young child screened for fear of the stigma of a mental health diagnosis. While some controversy among early childhood and mental health professionals about mental health screening for young children exists about when screening should take place and by whom, the bottom line is that a child needs nurturing, responsive, and consistent caregiving by a trusted caregiver in order to have the strongest foundation for future emotional development. The early childhood professional can accomplish the role of nurturing caregiver even if they choose not to be part of the screening process; regardless, providing referral information to parents for early intervention services is paramount.

All children, regardless of their development, gain from early childhood programs that promote exploration, self-regulation, social competence, and expression of feelings among other emotional competencies. The caregiver and educator need to promote emotional competence with their practices, child-care activities, physical and emotional environmental set up, and routines. The following are six important tools that early childhood practitioners can employ to support a child's mental health.

Early Childhood Tools for Enhancing
A Child's Mental Health

1. Teach Children to Understand and Talk about Their Feelings

Encourage children to understand and talk about their own feelings and the feelings of others. It sounds simple but sometimes our own emotions get in the way when we are teaching. If a child frequently shows aggression to another child, our sympathy with the injured child may keep us from acknowledging the feelings of BOTH children (Croft and Hewitt, 2004). We need to be vigilant in acknowledging and encouraging expressions of feelings by children. By giving guidelines, modeling, and reinforcement, we can help children understand what their own feelings mean, and what the feelings of others mean to them. One of the best gifts we can give children is the ability to articulate what they are feeling without our judgment. So, when Jacob says "I hate you" to Kahlil, we can intervene with "What is making you mad right now?" As we help Jacob dissect his feelings and give him non-hurtful words to use, we can also ensure that Kahlil's feelings are honored by asking him to share how the encounter made him feel. When a child understands that he can tell a friend, "That makes me mad when you take my spot in line," then it becomes less necessary for him to strike out with words like "hate" or other name-calling. The ability to name a feeling permits children to truly engage one another in dialogue and in reflection.

Researchers believe a child learns to empathize with other's feelings only once they've experienced the same feelings. There is mastery here as well; children begin to see emotions expressed in others and know they have felt those same feelings, and with both their growth and responsive caregiving in a safe environment, they begin to become more sophisticated in their understanding of a whole range of feelings. For example, children at ages 3 to 4 years become aware of happy feelings, whereas at ages 3½ to 4 they recognize fear, and at ages 3 to 8 they can identify anger and sadness (Kaufmann, 2005). As children grapple with new emotions, the early childhood teacher and caregiver can acknowledge these feelings and also give them words to explain their feelings. (Strategies for teachers to use to help children identify feelings are found in Chapter 4). Children who can name and discuss their feelings are developing into emotionally competent children.

Sonya's mom said goodbye to her and walked out of the door of the center. As Sonya began to cry, Malyun walked over and hugged her friend. She said, "Do you want to use the paint table with me?"

The Center on the Social and Emotional Foundations for Early Learning at the University of Illinois has identified the characteristics of classrooms that foster an emotional vocabulary for young children, referred to as *emotional literacy.* There are several characteristics that need to be present in the environment in order to encourage and support emotional literacy:

- Photos of people with various emotional expressions are displayed around the room.

- Books about feelings are available in the book corner.

- Teachers label their own feelings.

- Teachers notice and label children's feelings.

- Teachers draw attention to how a child's peer is feeling.

- Activities are planned to teach and reinforce emotional literacy.

- Children are reinforced for using feeling words.

- Efforts to promote emotional vocabulary occur daily and across all times of the day. (Permission to reprint from the Center on the Social Emotional Foundations for Early

Learning at the University of Illinois with funding from the Department of Human Services, Administration for Children and Families, 2004).

In addition, early childhood programs can provide the opportunities for children to develop understanding and empathy for the feelings, ideas, and actions of others. Using "feelings" posters or flash cards serves several purposes; they can teach about basic facial expressions for younger children, help them recognize those feelings in themselves or others, and also normalize the expression of feelings, for example, people get angry sometimes, people are sad sometimes. Educators can use the posters as a stepping stone to talking about what you do with those "big" feelings, what kinds of reactions are okay and which ones might hurt others. "Feelings Lotto" sets are another game that can help children recognize facial expressions or common social interactions, or become familiar with feeling words. Another way to use games at activity time is to purchase board games made specifically for topics like anger management or conflict resolution. Extending a child's natural play into talking about feelings is another intuitive strategy. As a child is playing with her doll baby, pretending the baby is crying, the caregiver can ask, "What's the matter with baby? How can we help baby so he doesn't cry?" This natural interchange can help the child name a feeling, "Baby is sad because her mommy is gone," and come up with ways to comfort or alleviate the distress.

Intentional group activities can provide opportunities for teachers and providers to let children practice emotional competencies. Using role-playing masks (you can make or purchase) allow children to apply various emotional responses or reactions during dramatic play time. Skits written by teachers or students can help children act out various emotions in appropriate ways or in problem-solving ways. You can discuss as a large group how different events make children feel, like having a new baby brother. Use opportunities that arise to encourage children to help each other, like getting a bandage for another child's scraped knee. Talk about how helping someone else makes everyone feel. These teaching moments, whether intentional or spur-of-the-moment, are perfect for modeling and practicing emotional proficiencies.

Aiyan, 3, saw her friend Noah from across the room. She smiled and began to run over to him, tripping before she reached him. As she sat crying, Noah also began to cry, saying, "Aiyan fall down."

2. Use Child-First Language

Another key strategy for helping children achieve healthy emotional development is intentionality in the type of language we use in speaking to and about children. Child-first language is a popular concept in the disability world: talking about the child, as a person, first, then their disability. So, it is not an autistic child, but a child with autism. The autism is a descriptor of the child, part of the child, but not a definition of the child. The child is a whole, the sum of many parts. When we are working with children, the philosophy of seeing a child as a person, first, should permeate all of our conversations. Someone working in public school with children who were labeled "at risk" refused the label; he chose to refer to them as "at promise." How we see children and speak about them and to them makes a difference in how they see themselves. This is the foundation of a child's self-image. It is our obligation to make sure that our language moves them forward in their emotional growth, closer to self-confidence, altruism, friendship, empathy, and self-regulation. York and Coram talk about the power of language in their article "The Impact of Our Words" from *Today's School Readers* (2004):

What's the big deal about labels and how we use certain words and phrases? The big deal is that our words have the power to affect our self-image and to create a lifetime of success or failure. We tend to discount the impact of words because we cannot see or touch the words we use. Yet each word we choose contains a powerful image. No longer just theory, today neuroscience recognizes that our words, whether thought or spoken, are physical energy—electrochemical triggers or impulses that program the mind-body system with pictures and verbal commands. Read the words don't think of pink elephants and what comes to mind? Pink elephants! When we label students as difficult, at risk, or stubborn, they get the picture of that negative label in their brains and it becomes the model for their behavior. They also get the negative energy of our labels, better known as "bad vibes."

As we model child-first language, we intentionally show other children and adults that we respect each child as an individual. We do not allow ourselves to lapse into easy judgments that often follow labels; we make it a point to avoid promoting self-fulfilling prophecies about young children. We model inclusive, supportive language both for other staff and for the children in our care in order to support positive mental health development.

3. Support Secure Attachments with Children

A childcare provider is in a unique position to help a child feel secure and loved. We've seen in Chapter 1 how important consistent caregiving is for all children. Children can only learn trust when they have had secure attachments to primary caregivers; and build trust scaffolds to other important milestones, like exploration and independence. Positive mental health depends on having met a child's security needs. A child who is insecure in their environment will find it hard to explore, to look beyond their small space, to take a risk. This will in turn inhibit their ability to initiate relationships with others, hindering empathy and other social skills. Autonomy is a key building block in a toddler's emotional growth; it can only develop in an environment that is safe, secure, and consistent.

In young children, separations that occur between the child and parent at the child-care setting can be very upsetting to both parent and child. Stress caused by separation can be alleviated by the child-care provider by making sure a trusting relationship is being developed between the child and themselves. Balaban (2006) has coined the phrase "curriculum of trust" where caregivers understand and validate feelings of separation as part of typical development. She recommends a few tips for creating the trusting relationship, including making sure that a primary caregiver exists for every child in the program, ensuring that there's one person that the child can always rely on. In addition, it is helpful (when possible) if the family eases into childcare, by visiting the program and taking part in some of the activities before enrolling full time. Staff can help each child by being part of the ritual goodbyes with parents, helping each child know that feelings are okay, that they will be safe here, and that mom or dad will be back later. Finally, encourage families to bring familiar items from home that remind the child of their parent to keep at the center or family child care home. "When teachers and caregivers ease the separation process by building trust, they help children build competence, confidence, and self-assurance" (Balaban, 2006).

There are other mechanisms for helping young children feel secure and comfortable in the early childhood environment. For very young children, thumb sucking and pacifiers may offer self-soothing while a familiar blanket or stuffed animal can provide comfort even with environmental changes. Keeping a familiar "comfort article" can help a child maintain her feeling of security as transitions occur between home and childcare. Children will outgrow these security items as they mature in a setting that consistently offers a sense of safety and responsiveness. Caregivers must offer close supervision and monitoring in their setting so a child both sees the vigilance of care and also avoids dangers. Using supportive language affirms a child's sense of self-concept; this must include the validation of feelings, honor of culture, and reminder to the child that "I am not going anywhere," and "This is a safe place."

Three children in the toddler room were crying loudly. Miss Esme knelt down to talk to them, saying, "Did the loud sound scare you? It's okay, you're safe here with me. We're all safe here."

Children at different ages will experience fear in different ways. Very young children go through stages of stranger anxiety and, as children grow, they learn new fears based on their environment and their emotional growth. It's not uncommon for a toddler, for instance, to fear storms or loud sirens. As we support secure attachments with children, we can help them through these periods of fearfulness by first acknowledging the fear. Then, we can step in with other strategies if fear is persistent, like giving them a concrete solution. In *In Sickness and Health,* the authors suggest if a child has an irrational fear of ghosts, for example, then giving the child a pretend magic wand might be enough to help them through the scary time. Again, encouraging the use of words as children grow will help them verbalize their fears so providers can better meet their needs. A secure setting will help alleviate fears and provide the foundation necessary for a child to be able to step out of their comfort zone and explore, both physically and emotionally.

4. Building a Sense of Community for All Children

For some children, the early childhood setting may be the only place they do truly feel a sense of belonging. So for us, that role of building the community becomes even more important. We have the authentic opportunity for helping children connect and feel connected, and it is something that must happen in order for any child to be successful. Without a sense of belonging, a child will have difficulty learning altruism, wanting to do good just for goodness' sake, and giving up personal needs at times for their larger community. In addition, recent research indicates that strengthening the child's community ties and interpersonal relationships may increase resiliency for the child and family who have some mental health issues (Focal Point, 2006).

We need to help children feel like they belong to their child-care community, and are important members of it. A child's emotional well-being is tied to his feelings of security and safety and these are products of a healthy community. It is only in a community that children can realize their full potential (Katz and McClellan, 1997). The early childhood setting is a community, where all members should be encouraged to invest and contribute. Practical strategies for building community in your program include:

A. **Recording Daily Highlights**. Children report highlights at the end of the preschool day, something memorable or important to them. These highlights can be kept in a book or posted on a board in the classroom (Berul, 2005).

B. **Classroom Jobs**. Children share in the different classroom functions during the day or at the end of the day. Keep the tasks on a wall with their name by it and change it every few days.

C. **Photographs**. Children's photos can be part of the art center, where different projects can be done involving their photos.

D. Naming Songs. Singing songs with children's names within the songs, with each child in the classroom being named (Berul, 2005).

E. Community Visitors. Different members of the larger community can be invited in to explain how their jobs help others, including mail carriers, veterinarians, fire fighters.

F. Family Photos. Invite the children to bring pictures of their parents and grandparents, cousins or other important people in their lives.

G. Cultural Respect. Keep the child-care environment alive with celebrations of the diversity of children in the program. Talk about likenesses and differences. Invite people from the larger cultural community into your program to talk to the children about their culture and customs. Make sure all children have representation of their culture throughout the program including photos and books.

5. Tune into Children

A child benefits emotionally when the important people around him listen and respond to his actions, words, feelings, and needs. We call this "tuning into" a child; observing a child to see what they are experiencing, intuiting what might be needed by them, responding to the emotional cues given to us by the child. This means we suspend our own judgments about what we think a child should be doing or feeling and we empower the child by following their lead. Tuning into a child takes intentionality, practice, and a keen responsiveness on the part of the teacher or caregiver.

Child-care providers can practice the skill of tuning into a child by paying close attention to a child as he enters the program at the beginning of the day. What is his affect and mood today? What does he seem to be interested in first? Does he seem approachable or does he first need some time alone to warm up? The child-care provider can then determine if it is a good time to spend some one-on-one with the child, letting the child decide what they will play, how the play will advance, and when it will be over. The interaction of tuning into a child is empowering, helping him see that his ideas are important, are valued, and that he is worthy of respect. This is an important self-esteem booster!

One tried and true technique for tuning into a child is the Floor Time® model of Dr. Stanley Greenspan (1997). His approach builds emotional health in children by helping them learn better relating and communication skills. Floor Time® is both a philosophy and a technique. As a technique, it is a five-step approach to interacting with a child, one-on-one, where the child takes the lead and is empowered by the adult caregiver in choice-making. The five steps are:

1. Observation: observing what mood the child seems to be in, what he is currently engaged in.

2. Approach and Opening the Circle of Communication: After assessing the child's mood and interests, the caregiver approaches the child with appropriate gestures or language to begin a mutual interaction.

3. Follow the Child's Lead: Engaging with the child in whatever his play happens to be as a supportive partner.

4. Extend and Expand: supporting the child's play with comments and actions that do not intrude on the child's interpretation of the play.

5. Closing the Circle of Communication: builds on the child's two-way communication skills as he leads the play in other directions based on the extend and expand conversations.

As a philosophy, Floor Time® is an intentionality about tuning into the child, respecting his choices, and building on his own self-awareness and self-esteem. You can learn more about this technique at http://home.sprintmail.com/~janettevance/floor_time.htm or http://www.floortime.org/.

Callie took a bite of toast and then gave her toy animal Chummer a pretend bite. She continued to eat her breakfast, sharing bites. Her caregiver said, "Callie, does Chummer like peanut butter?" and Callie replied, "Nope."

6.Set Up the Environment for Success

Early childhood educators and caregivers have primary control over their environment and programming when considering a child's healthy development. It is important for caregivers to arrange the environment and daily schedule so that children are able to make decisions for themselves, read and tell stories for which children can decide endings, and set up activities that allow children to make choices as they are continually practicing or testing their autonomy. The environment should encourage children to extend their activities in ways they create, by having open-ended play materials, few transitions, and supportive staff. Since self-regulation skills are important, intentional practices within the program that help children learn how to wait by taking turns, or waiting patiently for help are necessary. Some strategies for this include using timers or creating a waiting list for the next turn, announcing transitions five minutes prior to their happening to give children a chance to think about what will happen next so they can adjust their plans, and using picture schedules or cue cards. Children need to feel secure in their environment and just as importantly, they need positive interactions with their parents and caregivers. Programming activities need to include opportunities for role playing of emotions, labeling feelings, writing about feelings, sharing with one another about what one is feeling. The staff, if educated to respect a child and his feelings and emotions, will support a child's sense of security.

The following guidelines will help early childhood educators examine their emotional and physical environment for healthy practices to promote emotional well-being:

1. Is the care given to children warm, responsive, sensitive and consistent?

2. Does the child have a nurturing relationship with at least one teacher or provider?

3. Does the early childhood educator or child-care provider have emotional supports present in their own lives?

4. Is the early childhood environment language-rich, including opportunities for reading, singing, listening and talking?

5. Are the early childhood play environments comprised of developmentally appropriate play materials that encourage exploration, creativity, and interaction with others?

6. Is the opportunity for tuning into each child available every day? Do children receive some measure of one-on-one time with a primary caregiver each day?

7. Does the program encourage mastery of key emotional development skills and support the growth of new skills?

Ensuring that these guidelines are consistently met by caregivers will create an environment that is nourishing and supportive of each child.

Support for Strong Emotions and Problem Solving

Sometimes, children will be experiencing emotions that are intense and difficult for them to understand or cope with. Caregivers can support a child through difficulties by offering an environment that assures that all expressions of feelings are okay, as long as everyone is safe. The following excerpt is a practical approach by Fred Rogers to helping children cope with overwhelming feelings:

The Mad That We Feel
Thoughts from Fred Rogers for Parents, Caregivers and Teachers

A 5-year-old boy once asked me, "What do you do with the mad that you feel when you feel so mad you could bite?" Listening to his question made me think about what anger means to children. One thing I heard in his question was a reminder that children can   have intense angry feelings, too. Their anger, like ours, comes as a reaction to other feelings–for example, when they feel small, inadequate, rejected, hurt, or disappointed. Those feelings are painful, and they are very much a part of childhood.

There was more in that boy's question, though, than just telling me there were times when he felt really mad. He seemed to want to find out how grownups manage their anger so they don't hurt anyone. "How does a person find control at angry times?" he was asking.

That can be an especially important concern for 5-year-olds. At that time in their lives children are working hard to find control over many kinds of impulses. They're old enough to recognize what they're supposed to do and not do, but their inner controls are not well developed. It can be hard for them to hold back their destructive urges when they're angry and upset.

That's probably one reason why so many young children are attracted to stories about heroes and villains. Those figures may often represent a "good" inside force which can win out over a "bad" inside force. Young children, with their shaky controls, cannot always be sure what the outcome of the good-bad struggle inside them will be, and it may reassure them to find the "good guy" winning time and time again.

That 5-year-old's question made me realize again that children want some concrete alternatives to biting, hitting, and hurting. What I told him was that different people find different ways to handle their anger. "For me," I said, "it helps to play loud on the piano or even just to say, 'I'm mad!'" Some children let out their anger by doing a kind of temper-tantrum dance or by running fast. Others scribble harsh lines with crayons or markers or make pictures of angry faces and angry things. A friend of ours set up a punching bag in the basement for one of his children to use—a child who needed a target for his anger other than his younger brother. In many families hammering nails or pounding clay or dough are acceptable.

Offering as many creative and constructive outlets as possible is an important way parents can help their children learn to cope with anger. Of course, the ways we ourselves express our anger will influence our children the most. That, as well as our reactions to depictions of anger in stories or television.

One very important thing parents can do in their children's early struggles with anger is to set limits: Losing control is scary for children, and it helps them feel safe when we adults are firm about what we will and will NOT allow. In setting those limits, though, we need to acknowledge children's right to be angry; it's only what they do with that anger that we're regulating. For example, if there's a new baby girl in the family, parents could offer an older brother some important help by saying, clearly and firmly, "I can understand that you're angry about the baby, but I can't let you hurt her." It could help to add: "I wouldn't let anyone hurt you either."

Anger is a difficult feeling for most people - painful to feel and hard to express. It can help us and our children to remind ourselves that having angry feelings is a part of being human, whether we like it or not. It's simply a fact that loveable people get angry sometimes. We can't expect our children never to be angry, any more than we can ask that of ourselves, but we can help them find healthy ways for them to deal with the mad that they feel ... and help them know the good feeling that comes with self-control. (Permission to reprint, May, 2006).

Wisdom from the Field

As children learn to recognize and respond to strong emotions, early childhood practitioners need to support them safely as they maneuver through the new or uncharted waters. One way to help children is to teach them methods to manage conflicts that may arise. Early childhood educators, in a teacher preparation program, shared strategies they use to encourage children to develop and implement conflict resolution skills. First, they recommend that staff learn not to intervene too quickly in children's conflicts; be there to guide them and tell them when their suggestions are well-thought out, encouraging problem-solving skill development. Toddlers and preschoolers may need some redirection from the caregiver as they look for solutions. When it is time for adult intervention, show children how they can talk out problems with their friends, giving them words and phrases to use. Discuss openly with the children having the conflict, "What do you think will work to solve this, what won't work, why?" This can help them reach an agreeable solution together. Older children can be encouraged to write their feelings out on paper and then brainstorm possible solutions to getting along in the situation. Another strategy that helps older children work it out themselves is a "solution kit," which can be a box that contains different solution scenarios. Children can be encouraged to go to the kit and select one, try it out, and if it doesn't work, try another. Another tried and true method for older children is SIGEP: STOP what you are doing, ISOLATE what the problem is, GENERATE solutions, EVALUATE ideas, PUT ideas into action. You can help the children using SIGEP by making an easel pad available for writing their ideas down. Staff intervention is necessary when children aren't able to get to a workable solution or a child is in danger of harm. These strategies are easy to implement in an early childhood setting and are necessary because conflict resolutions skills are an important foundation for positive mental health growth. Proficiency in problem solving is needed by children in order to develop healthy relationships with others, including friends and caregivers.

Summary

The interventions and strategies outlined in this chapter can serve as positive supports for helping each child reach their potential for emotional health. There are many factors outside of the control or influence of the early childhood program that will have an impact on positive mental health, so we must concern ourselves as caregivers and teachers on the elements in a child's life for which we do have influence. Our interactions, our relationships, and our environments are key dynamics in helping children learn about themselves and their relationship to the world around them in a positive way.

Key Points:

1. The early years are the best time to intervene on behalf of children; we can impact their future with quality, responsive caregiving and early screening for emotional disorders.
2. By providing guidelines, modeling, and reinforcement, we can help children understand what their own feelings mean, and what the feelings of others mean to them.

3. When we model child-first language, we intentionally show other children and adults that each child is respected as an individual.

4. Children can only learn trust when they have had secure attachments to primary caregivers, building trust scaffolds to other important milestones, like exploration and independence.

5. The early childhood setting is a community, where all members should be encouraged to invest and contribute.

6. A child benefits emotionally when the important people around him listen and respond to his actions, words, feelings, and needs; we call this "tuning into" a child.

7. It is important for caregivers to arrange the environment and daily schedule so that children are able to make decisions for themselves, read and tell stories for which children can decide endings, and set up activities that allow children to make choices as they are continually practicing or testing their autonomy.

8. As children learn to recognize and respond to strong emotions, early childhood practitioners need to safely support them as they maneuver through the new or uncharted waters.

References

Ahn, H. (2005, Jan). Child care teachers' strategies in children's socialization of emotion. *Early Child Development & Care,* 175(1), 49.

Ainsworth, M. & Bowlby, J. (1965). *Child care and the growth of love.* London: Penguin Books.

Balaban, N. (2006, November). Easing the separation process for infants, toddlers, and families. *Young Children.*

Berk, L. (1997). *Child development.* Needham, MA: Allyn & Bacon.

Berul, M. (2005). Handout on *More Ideas for Building a Preschool Community.* NAEYC presentation December, 2005.

Bornstein, M., Chun-Shin, H. Gist, N., & Haynes, M. (2006, February). *Early Child Development & Care, 176(*2), 129-15.

Bromwich, R. (1997). *Working with families and their infants at risk.* Austin, TX: Pro-Ed.

Brouette, S. (2004, January/February). Aesthetics in the Classroom Setting. *Child Care Information Exchange.*

Campbell, S., Spieker, S., Burchinal, M., and Poe, M. (2006, August). Trajectories of aggression from toddlerhood to age 9 predict academic and social functioning through age 12. *Journal of Child Psychology & Psychiatry, 47*(8).

Cellitti, A. (2006). *In sickness and health: Mental health of toddlers in childcare.* Harbor Springs, MI: Healthy Child Publications.

Consortium Connections. (2006, Fall). University of Minnesota, 15(2).

Cook, A. (2007). Complex Trauma in Children and Adolescents. *Focal Point, 21*(1).

Croft, C. & Hewitt, D. (2004) *Children and challenging behavior: Making inclusion work.* Farmington, MN: Sparrow Media Group.

Glasser, H. & Easley, J. (1998). Transforming the difficult child. Vaughan Printing: Nashville: TN.

Greenspan, S. (1997). *Floor time, tuning in to each child.* New York: Scholastic.

Groves, B. (2007, winter). *Early Intervention as Prevention: Addressing Trauma in Young Children.* Focal Point.

Hawley, T. (2000). *Starting smart: How early experiences affect brain development.* Ounce of Prevention Fund and ZERO TO THREE.

Hesse, P. (2005). Conference Presentation "Supporting Children's Emotional Development in Schools and Communities." (December, 2005). National Association for the Education of Young Children Annual Conference.

In Harm's Way: Aiding Children Exposed to Trauma. (2005). Issue Brief No. 23, Grantmakers in Health: Denver, CO.

Johnson, K., Knitzer. J. (2006). *Early Childhood Comprehensive Systems that Spend Smarter: Maximizing Resources to Serve Vulnerable Children.* National Center for Children in Poverty: Columbia University, Mailman School of Public Health.

Joseph, G., Strain, P. Building Positive Relationships with Young Children. The Center on the Social and Emotional Foundations for Early Learning. Accessed online 2004: www.csefel.uiuc.edu: University of Illinois at Urbana-Champaign.

Kaiser, B, Sklar, J. (2003). *Challenging Behavior in Young Children.* Boston: Allyn and Bacon.

Karr-Morse, R., Wiley, M. (1997). *Ghosts from the Nursery: Tracing the Roots of Violence.* New York: Atlantic Monthly Press.

Katz, L., McClellan, D. (1997). *Fostering Children's Social Competence: The Teacher's Role.* Washington, D.C.: NAEYC.

Kaufmann, L. (2005). Beautiful minds. *Initiative Quarterly,* 11-17.

Koralek, D. (1999). For Now and Forever. Lewisville, NC: Kaplan Press.

"Mental Health," Microsoft® Encarta® Online Encyclopedia 2006. http://encarta.msn.com © 1997-2006 Microsoft Corporation.

Mr. Roger's Neighborhood http://pbskids.org/rogers/parents/parentmadfeelings.html © 2006 Family Communications, Inc., Used with permission.

National Center on Birth Defects and Developmental Disabilities. Accessed on 1/11/05 at http://www.cdc.gov/ncbddd/autism/actearly/default.htm

National Child Traumatic Stress Network, (2004). *Children and Trauma in America. A Progress Report of the National Child Traumatic Stress Network.* Durham, N.C. NECTAC Clearinghouse on Early Intervention and Early Childhood Special Education. (2005). *The impact of Abuse, Neglect and Foster Care Placement on Infants, Toddlers and Young Children: Selected Resources.* Compiled by Shaw, E., and Goode, S. Chapel Hill: NECTAC.

Peth-Pierce, R. (2001). *A Good Beginning: Sending America's Children to School with the Social and Emotional Competence They Need to Succeed.* Chapel Hill: University of North Carolina.

Phillips, D. (1987). *Quality in Child Care: What Does the Research Tell us?* Washington D.C.: NAEYC.

Quality, Compensation, and Affordability. (1995). NAEYC Position Statement. Washington, D.C.: NAEYC

Saffrin, J. Kilian, M. (2005). Crimes of the Heart. *Initiative Quarterly,* p. 42.

Schweinhart, L. J. Montie, Z. Xiang, W. S. Barnett, C. R. Belfield & M. Nores. (2005). *The High/Scope Perry Preschool Study Through Age 40.* Ypsilanti, MI: High/Scope Press.

Social-Emotional Development in Young Children. (2003). A Guide developed by the Michigan Department of Community Health: Division of Mental Health Services to Children and Families.

Sparling Meunier, K., Crooms, (2006). J. National Association for Education of Young Children Annual Conference, Atlanta, GA.

Spenciner, L., Appl, Dolores. Presentation at 2006 Division for Early Childhood National Conference: The Teacher's Role in Expanding Children's Learning Opportunities: Promoting Positive Social Environments.

Stephens, K. (2002). *Parenting Exchange.* Friendship Skills Library #4.

Strengthening social support. (2006, winter). *Focal Point,* Portland State University, Portland, OR, 21(1).

Thompson, R. contributing editor. (2001). *The Future of Children: Caring for Infants and Toddlers.* Vol. 11, No. 1, Spring/Summer 2001. Los Altos, CA: The David and Lucille Packard Foundation.

Traumatic stress/child welfare. (2007, winter). Focal Point. Portland State University, Portland, OR, 22(1).

Turecki, S. (2000). "The Difficult Child." Bantam Dell Publishing U.S. Dept of Education : http://www.ed.gov (accessed April 20, 2007).

Warhol, J. (1998). *New Perspectives in Early Emotional Development.* Johnson & Johnson Pediatric Institute, Ltd. Pediatric Round Table series.

Wittmer, D., Honig, A. (1994). *Encouraging Positive Social Development in Young Children.* Young Children, July.

Wolfe, B. (2004). St. John's Institute on Inclusion. St. John's University Presentation, St. John's University, Minnesota.

"Young Children." July, 1994.

York, M., Coram, C. "The Impact of Our Words." *Today's School.* March/April, 2004. Zero to Three. Volume 23:4, 2003.

Zero to Three. www.zerotothree.org.

Appendix:

National Mental Health Resources

American Academy of Child & Adolescent Psychiatry (AACAP)
3615 Wisconsin Avenue NW
Washington, DC 20016-3007
(800) 333-7636
www.aacap.org

American Association of Children's Residential Centers
51 Monroe Place, Suite 1603
Rockville, MD 20850
(301) 738-6460
www.aacrc-dc.org

American Psychiatric Association (APA)
1000 Wilson Boulevard, Suite 1825
Arlington, VA 22209-3901
(703) 907-7300
www.psych.org

American Psychological Association
Office of Public Affairs
750 1st Street NE
Washington, DC 20002-4242
(800) 374-2721
www.apa.org

Anxiety Disorders Association of America (ADAA)
8730 Georgia Avenue, Suite 600
Silver Spring, MD 20910
(240) 485-1001
www.adaa.org

Association for Treatment & Training in the Attachment of Children (ATTACh)
P.O. Box 11347
Columbia, SC 29211
(866) 453-8224
www.attach.org

Autism Society of America
7910 Woodmont Avenue, Suite 300
Bethesda, MD 20814-3067
(800) 3AUTISM (328-8416)
www.autism-society.org

Bazelon Center for Mental Health Law
1101 15th Street NW, Suite 1212
Washington, DC 20005-5002
(202) 467-5730
www.bazelon.org

Center for Mental Health Services (CMHS) Knowledge Exchange Network (KEN)
P.O. Box 42490
Washington, DC 20015
(800) 789-2647
www.mentalhealth.org

Child & Adolescent Bipolar Foundation (CABF)
1187 Wilmette Avenue P.M.B. #331
Wilmette, IL 60091
(847) 256-8525
www.bpkids.org

Children & Adults with Attention- Deficit / Hyperactivity Disorder (ChADD)
8181 Professional Place, Suite 201
Landover, MD 20785
(800) 233-4050
www.chadd.org

Depression & Bipolar Support Alliance
730 North Franklin Street, Suite 501
Chicago, IL 60610-7224
(800) 826-3632
www.dbsalliance.org

Depression & Related Affective Disorders Association (DRADA)
Meyer 3-181
600 North Wolfe Street
Baltimore, MD 21287-7381
(410) 955-4647 www.drada.org

Federation of Families for Children's Mental Health
1101 King Street, Suite 420
Alexandria, VA 22314
(703) 684-7710

Minnesota Association for Children's Mental Health (MACMH)
165 Western Avenue N, Suite 2,
St. Paul, MN 55102
651-644-7333
1-800-528-4511 (in MN only)
www.macmh.org

National Alliance for the Mentally Ill (NAMI)
Colonial Place Three
2107 Wilson Boulevard, Suite 300
Arlington, VA 22201
(800) 950-NAMI (6264)
www.nami.org

National Association of Anorexia Nervosa & Associated Disorders (ANAD)
P.O. Box 7
Highland Park, IL 60035
(847) 831-3438 www.anad.org

National Center for Learning Disabilities
381 Park Avenue S, Suite 1401
New York, NY 10016
(888) 575-7373
www.ld.org

National Clearinghouse for Alcohol & Drug Information
11426-28 Rockville Pike, Suite 200
Rockville, MD 20852
(800) 729-6686
www.health.org

National Information Center for Children & Youth with Disabilities
(NICHCY)
P.O. Box 1492
Washington, DC 20013
(800) 695-0285
www.nichcy.org

National Institute of Mental Health (NIMH)
NIH Neuroscience Center
6001 Executive Boulevard
Rm 8184, MSC 9663
Bethesda, MD 20892-9663
(301) 443-4513
www.nimh.nih.gov

National Mental Health Association
2001 N Beauregard St.,
12th Floor
Alexandria, VA 22311
(800) 969-NMHA(6642)
www.nmha.org

Obsessive-Compulsive Foundation
676 State Street
New Haven, CT 06511
(203) 401-2070
www.ocfoundation.org

Prevent Child Abuse America
200 South Michigan Ave.,
17th Floor
Chicago, IL 60604
(312) 663-3520
www.preventchildabuse.org

Substance Abuse & Mental Health Services Administration (SAMHSA)
US Department of Health & Human Services
5600 Fishers Lane
Rockville, MD 20857
(301) 443-1563
www.samhsa.gov

Index:

About the Author

Cindy Croft is Director of the Center for Inclusive Child Care in St. Paul, Minnesota. The Center for Inclusive Child Care is a comprehensive resource network for promoting and supporting inclusive early childhood and school-age programs and practitioners with training and consultation, and other resources at www. inclusivechildcare.org. She also is faculty at Concordia University and Minneapolis Community and Technical College and teaches for the Minnesota on-line Eager To Learn program. She has her M.A. in Education with an Early Childhood Emphasis. She co-edited *"Children and Challenging Behavior: Making Inclusion Work"* with Deborah Hewitt.